EX LIBRIS

A SUSSEX GUIDE

BLOOMSBURY IN SUSSEX

SIMON WATNEY

Illustrated by
BARBARA CHILDS

SNAKE RIVER PRESS

SNAKE RIVER PRESS

Book No 6
Books about Sussex for the enthusiast

Published in 2020 by
SNAKE RIVER PRESS
South Downs Way, Alfriston, Sussex BN26 5XW
www.snakeriverpress.co.uk

ISBN 978-1-906022-25-9

This book was conceived, designed and produced by
SNAKE RIVER PRESS

Copyright © Snake River Press Limited 2007
Text © Simon Watney
Illustration © Barbara Childs

All rights reserved. No part of this book may be reproduced
in any form without written permission from the publisher.

The publishers and authors have done their best to ensure
the accuracy and currency of all information at the date of preparation.
Readers who intend to rely on the information to undertake any activity
should check the current accuracy. The publishers and authors accept
no responsibility for any loss, injury or inconvenience sustained by the
reader as a result of information or advice contained in this book.

ART DIRECTOR & PUBLISHER *Peter Bridgewater*
EDITORIAL DIRECTOR *Viv Croot*
EDITOR *Robert Yarham*
PAGE MAKEUP *Richard Constable & Chris Morris*
ILLUSTRATOR *Barbara Childs*
CONSULTANT *Lorraine Harrison*

This book is typeset in Perpetua & Gill Sans,
two fonts designed by Eric Gill

Printed and bound in Poland

DEDICATION

For Kay

CONTENTS

INTRODUCTION
6

THE BLOOMSBURY GROUP
10

THE SUSSEX CONNECTION
24

FIRLE & ASHEHAM
28

MONKS HOUSE
38

CHARLESTON
56

BERWICK CHURCH
79

BRIEF LIVES
89

BIBLIOGRAPHY
90

FOOTNOTES
94

INDEX
96

INTRODUCTION

everything has significance
PATTI SMITH, 2006

This is a book about a particular group of London-based artists and writers and the temporary homes they established in East Sussex in the early years of the 20th century, before finally settling for good in the late 1930s. Certainly it was the desire to find a bolt-hole far away from London which first drew Virginia Stephen to take a one-year lease on a newly built and rather ugly semi-detached house in the village of Firle early in 1911, a year before her marriage to Leonard Woolf. However, it was quiet and remote and while staying there in September of the same year she came across the house of her dreams only a few miles away. This was Asheham House in Beddingham, set back from the winding road between Lewes and Newhaven. Initially she shared the lease with her older sister, the artist Vanessa Bell; they had a house-warming party in February 1912.

This was the largely unplanned start of an immensely productive and life-changing relationship for both the sisters and their closest friends and family with the remarkable and still largely unspoiled stretch of countryside which lies between the River Ouse and the wide, gaunt, sky-reflecting estuary of Cuckmere Haven, immortalised in a 1939 watercolour by Eric Ravilious in the collection of Eastbourne Art Gallery. Four years after taking on Asheham Vanessa moved on to Charleston, an empty farmhouse at the foot of Firle Beacon just east of Beddingham, and the pattern of the rest of their lives was fixed.

It is important to recognise that these were not 'second homes' in the early 21st-century sense of the phrase, and it should be appreciated that both sisters turned towards Sussex just before and during World War I with some considerable practical urgency. For the first few years, Asheham was very much a convalescence home for Virginia Woolf, who for most of 1913 and 1914 was slowly recovering from a severe mental breakdown. Meanwhile Charleston was taken on in 1916 in the context of a rather different emergency when, as a conscientious objector, the 31-year-old artist Duncan Grant was required to undertake demanding farm-labour and Vanessa Bell took charge of the grim situation confronting not only her most intimate and cherished friend and colleague, but also herself – now a 37-year-old single mother with two small children, long separated from her philandering husband Clive, whom she had married ten years earlier, and with whom she remained on cautiously friendly terms.

In the course of time, both houses evolved into places where the sisters could work, raise children and entertain in peace away from their London homes, which were generally rented and shared with an ever-changing population of friends, family and servants. This must have made life exciting but hardly ideal for the undertaking of quiet, concentrated creative work. When the lease on Asheham came to an end in 1919 Virginia and Leonard bought Monks House in the nearby village of Rodmell, which remained their Sussex home for the rest of their lives.

For both sisters this new domestic expansion into Sussex provided a privacy they lacked in London and which they both equally craved. Against the dramatically undulating backdrop of the broad, rounded South Downs they established households in which they pioneered a wholly modern vision of art and literature, while at the same time anticipating many of the most important changes in later 20th-century personal and social relations which continue to be felt today. Neither Charleston nor Monks House were luxurious by any standards and, in the early years, life in both houses was spartan in the extreme, but over time their furnishings and decorations came uniquely to express the spirit of their remarkably creative and innovative occupants.

As early photographs show, life at Charleston and Monks House initially involved few creature-comforts.[1] It should, however, be understood that the living standards to which their Bloomsbury inhabitants aspired were very different from the expectations of those who regard luxurious domestic technology as the highest form of cultural achievement, and who would consider the earth closets and austere, chilly bathrooms of Monks House and Charleston evidence of unthinkable backwardness.

Both houses were gradually made more comfortable, but while Charleston is now an Edenic vision of itself almost exactly as it appeared a few years before the death of Duncan Grant in 1978, Monks House is not as it was in Virginia Woolf's lifetime, and is much changed even from its appearance when Leonard Woolf died in 1968. Most of the Woolfs' books and pictures have gone, leaving the decorated framework of the house and some of its original furniture. Yet to a great extent it still embodies Bloomsbury taste, quite unlike any other style of 20th-century decoration and instinct with the sensibility of its former owners.

To take one example, I would single out for attention the remarkable sequence of dust-jackets designed by Vanessa Bell for her sister's books, self-published by the Hogarth Press which Virginia and Leonard Woolf had founded in 1917, from *Monday or Tuesday* in 1921 to the many posthumous publications supervised by her surviving husband, up to *Granite and Rainbow* in 1958. One might supplement this sequence with Duncan Grant's beautiful covers for the five volumes of the Diaries of Virginia Woolf published between 1976 and 1982. Taken together they provide a most eloquent summary of an entire lifestyle centrally concerned with books and the visual arts. Using starkly simplified forms which emphasise the flatness of the page, Duncan and Vanessa's dust-jackets provide self-sufficient visual equivalents rather than illustrations. Reticent, poetic and highly decorative, they remain effective ambassadors on behalf of an entire philosophy of life and the visual arts.

This short book does not set out to retell the stories of the lives of the central figures of Bloomsbury, for that is by now a well-trodden path. Nor does it offer a complete picture of the art of Vanessa Bell and Duncan Grant as it focuses mainly on their decorative work. Rather, I want to concentrate on the appearance of the homes they made for themselves in Sussex and the uses to which they were put. As the character of Mrs Swithin murmurs in Virginia Woolf's last novel:

We have other lives, I think, I hope (...) We live in others (...) We live in things.[2]

My main attention is thus on the things they made, and what their homes tell us about their makers and their remarkable contribution to the making of modern Britain. To an unusual extent the homes and studios of the members of the Bloomsbury group were integral to their artistic and literary achievements, and this book is chiefly about their highly distinctive tastes in furniture and fabrics, carpets and ceramics, gardens and kitchens. As Noel Annan observed,

> they embodied more than any other movement the English response to the revolution in art and morals that we call Modernism.[3]

In a country which has shown consistently little respect for the preservation of artists' homes, both Charleston and Monks House are now open to the public, and together with the murals and other decorations in nearby Berwick church, they provide a unique picture of the early Modernist cultural and personal vision associated with Bloomsbury. Their enduring significance is well reflected by the poet and singer Patti Smith's recent description of Charleston as a house that feels 'like home', where art 'was part of everyday living', a place where 'everything has significance – a humble box, a shell'.[4]

Footnotes: *All footnotes are grouped together at the back of this book on pages 94–95. The names Virginia Woolf, Leonard Woolf and Vanessa Bell are abbreviated throughout to their initials.*

Acknowledgements

I would like to thank the following for their help and advice: Mrs Anne Olivier Bell, Mark Divall (Charleston), Wendy Hitchmough (Charleston), Mrs Sandra Lummis, Michael Moon, Karen Watson (University of Sussex Library, Special Collections), and Caroline Zoob (Monks House). Like all historians of Bloomsbury art I am greatly indebted to Richard Shone's guides to Charleston and Berwick church. I should also like to thank my partner Glyn for all his support.

Simon Watney, 2006

THE BLOOMSBURY GROUP
A LARGELY IMAGINARY GROUP OF PERSONS

A collection of immensely gifted and influential writers, artists and others, including the art critic Roger Fry and the economist Maynard Keynes, the Bloomsbury group pioneered and shaped many of the most important and attractive aspects of modern British life. They recognised the need for the repeal of cruel and discriminatory Victorian legislation, but did not equate this with the rather different task of changing public attitudes towards marriage, child-rearing and personal relationships, as well as to art and design.

In order to understand anything about Bloomsbury we need to think back to the Indian summer of late-Victorian imperial England in which its members grew up: a prosperous but deeply class-divided country bursting with xenophobic and chauvinistic self-confidence, in which oxen still toiled in the fields at the foot of the South Downs, and the Lord Chamberlain was authorised to censor all texts for public theatrical performance in order that they should conform to the most elaborate and exactingly hypocritical standards of public decency. It was a world of sharp double standards between men and women, where homosexuality was made entirely illegal in 1885, and in many respects the major institutions regulating public life had more in common with the age of Queen Anne than our own.

It was against this suffocating background that we must picture the Bloomsbury group's early exodus from London. Few of them came from conventionally happy homes, and none had been at ease with their parents. The early years of the Stephen sisters were largely overshadowed by successive waves of illness, family losses and harsh treatment by their father and step-brothers after the early deaths of their mother and beloved older step-sister. All were dissatisfied with the rigours and rituals of the late Victorian middle-class household and its emotionally stultifying effects. From these, of course, they never entirely escaped, however unorthodox their subsequent lives may have been by the standards of most of their contemporaries.

In 1964 Leonard Woolf explained with characteristic insight that the term Bloomsbury 'was and is currently used as a term – usually of abuse – applied to a largely imaginary group of persons'.[1] Writing to her husband in 1931, Vanessa Bell drew his attention to an article in *The Times*,

> *sniping at Bloomsbury. I really think it is time someone pointed out that Bloomsbury was killed by the war (...) not that it matters much, only one wonders what the cause is. Is it really hatred of Roger [Fry], or what? I can't think that anyone in their senses can now lump Duncan [Grant] and Roger together as artists or influences.*[2]

Yet lump them all together they did, and continue so to do.

Born in the 1870s and 1880s, the members of Bloomsbury were formed before World War I and were thus of a generation described by Virginia Woolf in her final novel who 'were neither one thing nor the other, neither Victorians nor themselves'[3]. The men had first met as undergraduates at Cambridge, soon mixing closely with one another's families and other friends. They famously honoured friendship, modesty, self-criticism, sexual honesty, creativity and intellectual enquiry, while not failing to recognise the ways in which these qualities may come into conflict. There was, however, no blueprint for how they might put all this into practice in their own lives.

Opposed to demagoguery and fanaticism of all kinds, opposed indeed to the sound of voices raised in anger, they were generally given to understatement, reason, dialogue and irreverent good humour. In spite of their many differences they stood collectively against the deep strain of puritanism within British life and culture, and expressed themselves with vivacious candour, never more serious than when telling jokes. Moreover as Quentin Bell has suggested, it is doubtful whether any English group 'had ever been so radical in its rejection of sexual taboos'.[4] Many of these values may be found reflected in the surviving Sussex homes of the original central figures of the group, and the nature and significance of their unique visual style is my central theme.

Certainly not everyone in Bloomsbury got on with one another. For example, Lytton Strachey never liked Roger Fry and many of the group became gradually distanced from Maynard Keynes, while Clive Bell and Leonard Woolf were never in any real sense friends. And of course they could get on one another's nerves from time to time, like all mere mortals. They did, however, generally feel a strong sense of Europe as 'a family of nations, bound to one another by the ethical standards of an old and common civilization', as Leonard Woolf once put it.[5]

Futhermore, the members of Bloomsbury shared an exhilarating sense peculiar to the handful of years before the outbreak of World War I that immense social change for the better was imminent, of which the arts were understood as a kind of litmus test. This went hand in hand with a general dislike of things Victorian. However, as the 20th century progressed, this early optimism was gradually replaced by a darker fear that the war had fatally undermined the entire inherited basis of European civilisation. With this perception went an increasingly pessimistic awareness that the Treaty of Versailles of 1919 had led directly to the rise of Hitler and, moreover, that those in power had by consistent policies of appeasement betrayed their own country by defending the Nazis as bulwarks against Soviet communism. Few commentaries on the rise of the dictators have stood the test of time as depressingly well as that of Leonard Woolf written in Rodmell in the late 1930s.[6]

Vanessa Bell and Virginia Woolf

At this point it seems helpful to turn briefly to the relationship between Vanessa Bell and Virginia Woolf whose personalities lay at the heart of Bloomsbury, which is perhaps best understood as two closely overlapping circles of friends each focused on one of the two sisters. Nor should one forget the extreme rarity of significant creative gifts being shared by siblings, particularly in such different fields as painting and writing. For all his romantic fascination, Bramwell Brontë was hardly a great artist, and apart from the artist Dante Gabriel Rossetti and his poet sister Christina, no real parallel springs to mind.

Born respectively in 1879 and 1881, Vanessa Bell and Virginia Woolf were the daughters of Sir Leslie Stephen (*1832-1904*) and his second wife Julia Jackson Duckworth, who already had three children by her first marriage. She also had a further two sons with Sir Leslie, a distinguished author and critic and the founding editor of *The Dictionary of National Biography*, whose first wife Harriet was the youngest daughter of the novelist William Thackeray. Vanessa and Virginia thus grew up in an intensely literary household, dominated by a father who became increasingly tyrannical after Julia's death in 1895. Her loss was partly assuaged by their half-sister Stella who assumed many of Julia's thankless domestic responsibilities before her escape through marriage, closely followed by her own tragically premature death in 1897.

Their adolescence was largely blighted by what Quentin Bell has described as their father's 'savage, self-pitying emotional blackmail (…) of which they spoke but which they never made public'.[7] In the seven long dark years between Stella's death and that of their father in 1904, they were also plagued by the overly intrusive attentions of their two considerably older half-brothers. Small wonder then that they eventually struck out on their own in a spirit of defiant rejection of the standards of conventional Victorian family life which had caused them both such unnecessary suffering. On their father's death, they quit the gloomy family home in South Kensington in favour of a new life in Gordon Square in the geographically and socially distant London district of Bloomsbury.

The subsequent history of the Bloomsbury group was largely the legacy of these two remarkable sisters, artists of the first calibre, both deeply wounded by their early life to which was added the loss of their beloved brother Thoby Stephen in 1906 at the age of 26. Both sisters were profoundly self-critical and at the same time contemptuous of self-pity. Having early on defined their future respective careers as an artist and a writer, both were immensely productive, hard-working and self-motivated, and were equally committed to the highest artistic standards, sometimes at considerable cost to themselves and to those around them, who recognised something of the extraordinary nature of their personal and artistic achievements, not least in having survived the emotional rigours of their upbringing.

Together the sisters set the tone of Bloomsbury. Theirs was essentially a double-act: Vanessa the calm, dry, quiet ironist contrasting with Virginia's marvellously fanciful and imaginative personality which survives best in her incomparably amusing, gossipy, shrewd, worldly letters. Something of their mutual and complementary sense of humour may perhaps be lost on those of a more literal disposition in these over-literal times, but it is impossible not to respond to their seriousness about their work, which they communicated with the lightest of touches and the utmost modesty.

Virginia's mental fragility and periodic breakdowns were contrasted by them both to Vanessa's immense strength of will, expressed from early sisterly nicknames to an increasingly elaborate personal mythology which came to be widely accepted by their friends. Vanessa doubtless accepted her given persona as an archaic mother-goddess, part Aphrodite, part Demeter, in so far as it accorded well with her evident unwillingness to get involved in types of intellectual debate and enquiry which held no interest for her. Yet as Jane Dunn points out, it also locked her securely 'into the straitjacket of sanity'.[8] Regarded by almost everyone around her as the personification of female authority and wisdom, Vanessa's vulnerability was rarely acknowledged. It was as if Virginia had her older sister's depression for her, which may be one reason why Vanessa often appears strangely incurious in her letters about the reasons for her sister's problems.

This was a dangerous area for Vanessa, since to delve too deeply into the causes of Virginia's difficulties threatened to raise issues about her own past which she clearly much preferred to forget. Vanessa's frequently stated disinterest in the subject matter of art was in some ways a similarly convenient pose borrowed from Roger Fry in order to protect her privacy and to pre-empt further discussion of her inner life. Vanessa's goddess status was moreover a fiction which in some respects reversed the truth, since in many respects she was at least as harmed by her life-long struggles to deny even the acknowledgement of the constant threat of depression as her sister was by a more outwardly symptomatic mental illness. Moreover, Virginia was in many ways more of a fighter, as she herself eventually came to realise.[9]

To her own daughter Vanessa seemed much closer than Virginia to the everyday world.

> *By comparison she was calm, like a pool on which the coloured leaves slowly change their patter. She accepted, rather than protested; was passive, rather than avid. She did not care deeply about abstract ideas, and was led by her sensibilities rather than her intellect. In theory she supported rationalism, though her own acts were usually compulsive. She instinctively limited her life to the two things she cared for most: her painting and her family. The wider world seemed to her to threaten these two points (…) Love, with her, was an exclusive rather than an inclusive emotion; there was a chosen circle round which she planted a high palisade that cast its shadows both on those without and those within (…) Virginia danced round her like a dragon-fly round the water-lily, darting in to attack before Vanessa could take action (…) She sat and sewed or painted or listened (…) Even if she said little, there emanated from her an enormous power, a pungency like the smell of crushed sage. She presided, wise yet diffident, affectionate and a little remote, full of unquenchable spirit. Her feelings were strong, and words seemed to her inadequate. She was content to leave them to her sister and to continue painting.*[10]

However, as Frances Spalding comments, Vanessa may have done

> *less for the women's cause than her sister and yet, judged by the standards of everyday behaviour, Vanessa was far more revolutionary (…) Her rejection of most of those habits and customs which curtailed the lives of other women of their class grew out of her belief in the absolute need for personal freedom.*[11]

This did not necessarily make for private happiness, and it is surely significant that neither sister married for reasons of conventional romantic love, and both spent their adult lives in sexless central relationships, if for different reasons and with different consequences for themselves and those around them. Nothing more clearly reveals the extent of their equal underlying vulnerability than the fact that they both slept for most of their adult lives on chastely single beds. Nor did worldly success or recognition come early for either of them. Virginia did not publish her first novel until the age of 37, and Vanessa was 43 at the time of her first one-woman show in 1923.

In this context one is mindful of Virginia Woolf's observation that 'We think back through our mothers if we are women',[12] and her unforgettable description of her own mother as a woman who

> *reversed those natural instincts which were so strong in her of happiness and joy in a generous and abundant life, and pressed the bitterest fruit only to her lips. She visited the poor, nursed the dying, and felt herself possessed of the true secret of life at last, which is still obscured from a few, that sorrow is our lot, and at best we can but face it bravely.*[13]

It is difficult not to feel pity for the children of such a remorselessly perfect being.

Much of Virginia Woolf's fiction involved a creative re-imagining of their shared past, taking Vanessa back to their childhood as a form of 'reality checking' as it were, and perhaps as much for her sake as for her own. Writing from France in 1927, Vanessa praised Virginia's recently published *To The Lighthouse* for providing a portrait of their mother in the person of Mrs Ramsay,

> *which is more like her to me than anything I could have conceived possible (…) It was like meeting her again with oneself grown up and on equal terms and it seems to me the most astonishing feat of creation.*[14]

Yet as Jane Dunn points out, while Vanessa regarded the character of Mrs Ramsay as a remarkable reincarnation of their mother, Roger Fry recognised in it 'a moving portrait of Vanessa', not least in her relentless need to control those around her.[15]

Given her background and history, it is not difficult to understand how Vanessa came to shelter behind a reputation of formidable strength in contrast with her younger sister's more evident fragility. However, both sisters were equally tortured by self-doubt and vulnerable to depression. Duncan Grant sacrificed much to the task of maintaining Vanessa's sanity, much as Leonard Woolf dedicated himself to Virginia's emotional welfare. In so far as Vanessa could accept mothering from anyone, she accepted it from him, and there is a deep gap in our understanding of Bloomsbury if we do not from the outset recognise her extreme inner vulnerability matched by her equally ferocious instinct to control those around her, from which Duncan and her children all suffered, albeit in different ways. Duncan doubtless greatly loved and esteemed Vanessa, but he never pretended that he was heterosexual, or made promises to her which might be held against him. To a considerable extent Duncan was her emotional prisoner, and intuitively recognising the reasons for her need to imprison him, did the best he could to soften her compulsive, self-inflicted role of disappointed suitor, over which she evidently had little control or understanding. Yet we should recognise that at the heart of Bloomsbury lay two remarkable, productive creative partnerships, which in the case of Duncan and Vanessa endured for more than half a century.

Bloomsbury Modernism

It is not my task in these pages to attempt to summarise the range of Bloomsbury's many public achievements, but it should be pointed out that on the whole the study of Bloomsbury has been heavily weighted towards the literary, reflecting the longstanding English tendency to belittle the visual arts, from which some members of Bloomsbury were themselves not always entirely immune. This situation is complicated by the fact that the painters of Bloomsbury were themselves modest and self-deprecating to a fault, and incapable of self-promotion.

Early Modernism was never a unified international 'movement'. On the contrary, it involved a wide range of responses forged in relation to local cultural traditions, whether in London or Amsterdam or St Petersburg, and it is absurd to try to judge them all by the same criteria.

Indeed, it is in the great variety of its many variant national styles that early Modernism seems, in retrospect, most exciting, and of these the version developed by the artists of Bloomsbury is every bit as valid and distinct as the Modernism of the De Stijl group in Holland, or the Section d'Or group in Paris. Nor was there any parallel elsewhere for the duration of the close creative dialogue between Vanessa Bell and Duncan Grant, which far too often goes unremarked or else is bizarrely understood as some kind of disqualification for taking them seriously, rather than making them and their work seem all the more interesting.

Vanessa Bell and Duncan Grant privately shared the highest possible artistic standards, and one can only admire Vanessa for never forgetting nor forgiving John Rothenstein's foolish throwaway comment on a visit to Charleston that Titian couldn't draw.[16] Indeed the whole history of Charleston is inseparable from the way in which Duncan and Vanessa felt safe with one another, away from their over-intellectual literary friends. For all her great respect of the intellect Virginia Woolf was well aware, as she points out in *Orlando*, that it 'often, alas, acts the cannibal among the other faculties so that often, where the Mind is biggest, the Heart, the Senses, Magnanimity, Charity, Tolerance, Kindliness, and the rest of them scarcely have room to breathe'.[17]

Consummate professionals to their fingertips, Vanessa Bell and Duncan Grant not only shared a passionate excitement when young about the latest developments in painting in Paris before 1914, they were both also deeply grounded in the history of their medium. Their letters to one another are packed with constant references to painters and paintings about which they shared a profoundly nourishing mutual passion. Art was the primary substance of their private world, and sustained much of their private dialogue, a passion they could share with nobody else with the same intensity. If he told her that something was the colour of the dress worn by St Helena in Veronese's great picture in the National Gallery, she would instantly and precisely know the pale silvery orange-pink to which he referred. Such dialogue is quite different to that of most writers and is available only to those for whom the visual arts are the most significant of all.

In 1929 Duncan and Vanessa decorated the dining-room at Penns-in-the-Rocks, the late-17th-century home of the literary hostess Lady Dorothy Wellesley at Withyham in Sussex. At the time the decor was widely admired but it was unfortunately dismantled after Lady Dorothy's death. The prevailing colours were, as usual in Bloomsbury decorations, muted, with grey-green walls, a pale grey ceiling and carpet, and a pink fireplace decorated with pale green circles. The furniture, painted predominantly pale salmon-pink and grey, included an octagonal dining-table with a set of matching cane-backed chairs, side-tables and a sideboard, presided over by six large figurative wall panels, three by each artist, including two large upright panels flanking the fireplace, and three more along one wall, with a smaller panel filling a corner.

The room was lit by alternating octagonal mirrors fixed above ground-glass wall-lights like modernist candle-sconces, matching a larger octagonal mirror above the fireplace, to great effect. Vanessa Bell's curtains were of pale mauve silk appliqué with yellow and orange and patches of glittering sequins. Sadly the five surviving decorated panels now in the Southampton Art Gallery provide little sense of the integrity of the overall scheme which, like all their best work, depended on the overall relations of walls, furniture and fittings, conceived as an ensemble for a particular house and client.

High up on the right side of the main hall of Brighton Art Gallery hangs a single large wall-panel painted by Duncan Grant, one of six designed for the interior of an imaginary Music Room exhibited at the Reid and Lefevre Gallery in London in 1932. Displayed too high, and out of alignment with its surroundings, it makes the same point. Bloomsbury decoration involved schemes for entire rooms, and individual elements were never intended to stand alone in this way. Some of their painted furniture is sufficiently autonomous to stand such treatment, yet essentially theirs was a carefully calculated style of overall decorative effect, generally designed for specific locations and to be seen *in situ*.

Primarily painters, the artists of Bloomsbury are sometimes blamed for not having been 'proper' designers, yet this is to spectacularly miss the point of their insistence on the artist's continued role as decorator and interior designer in the exhilarating early days of Modernism, and their refusal to hand everything over to architects. Born respectively in 1879 and 1885, Vanessa Bell and Duncan Grant were leading figures from the earliest phase of British modern art which was all but extinguished in the trenches of Flanders, only to be rediscovered by later generations. Although British in outlook and training, they shared a deep love and awareness of the wider traditions of European painting and the decorative arts. Insistently not pasticheurs, they were in many respects much more defiantly modern than most of their successors in the 1920s and 1930s. Hence the exasperated tone of Vanessa Bell's comment on the decorative arts in England:

where it seems to me one can never get away from all this fatal prettiness.[18]

With few exceptions their work in all media was generally conceived for comparatively small domestic environments. Hand-made, vibrant, sensual, life-affirming, and quite different from the mainstream industrialised and streamlined Art Deco style of the interwar years, their experimental modernism evolved in the hands and through the eyes of artists initially sensitised to the taste and outlook of the Arts and Crafts movement. Above all they wished as artists to reclaim the field of interior design and to extend their work beyond the field of easel-painting onto walls, and into fabrics, furnishings, ceramics and other elements in the domestic arena. In this central respect they were without peers or obvious precedents.

They felt themselves to be the heirs of an unbroken living tradition of decorative art in Britain, and their mood is rarely if ever elegiac, by contrast with the later work of younger artist-designers such as Edward Bawden, Eric Ravilious or Rex Whistler. Indeed the mood of their work is quite different from the exquisite updated rococo visions of so much fashionable art and design in the inter-war years. Bloomsbury art and decoration lacks any trace of the ironic stance of the Sitwell circle and their decorators, and was far removed from the inter-war nostalgia for the lifestyle associated with grand country houses.[19] This after all was precisely what the artists of Bloomsbury had resolutely turned their backs on. They were not out to revisit Brideshead, nor were they vulnerable to the siren charms of the Second Empire.

At the Omega Workshops in London between 1913 and 1919, Vanessa and Duncan had pioneered and anticipated most of the trends which would subsequently become widely fashionable and commercially successful in the fabrics and ceramics of the 1920s and 1930s. Much of their early decorative work derived from the geometric abstraction of Cubism, but this was always balanced by an equal emphasis on boldly drawn curvilinear patterns including leaves, plant-forms and simplified figurative elements. This can be seen if one compares their many surviving painted screens, or their later painted decorations in the dining room and the garden sitting-room at Charleston. It is surely significant that they did not turn to the production of wallpapers, preferring to work directly onto walls in a much more painterly fashion, albeit sometimes using stencils. This was in marked contrast to their commercially produced fabrics and ceramics.

The whole style of Bloomsbury's enthusiasm for the decorative arts derived from the optimism of Europe before World War I, which was very different from the outlook of younger inter-war designers. This was not evasion on their part; on the contrary, it involved and required a particular kind of heroism, immensely serious in its aims yet expressed in terms of great playfulness and humour. To appreciate this point one need only compare Bloomsbury's book-covers to the very different if delicious nostalgia-drenched style employed by Rex Whistler and others to adorn the Sitwells' many publications. In this respect Vanessa Bell remained a full-blooded experimental Modernist in her work for the Hogarth Press, right up to the late 1950s. There is never a trace of historical pastiche. In its way, her natural decorative vocabulary of big circles and radically simplified architectural forms (including swagged curtains) represented a dramatic paring down of the inherited style of 18th-century designer-decorators such as Robert Adam, but the effect could hardly be more different.

Bloomsbury decoration never employed the type of fussily detailed, illusionistic techniques found so often in mid-20th-century English decorative art, and aspired to a rather grander, simpler style, which always emphasised the surface of whatever was being decorated. Duncan Grant in particular had a strong feeling for the big gestures of baroque art, but this was always translated into his own distinctive style. The *commedia del arte* figures found so often in his later paintings and decorations were part of his everyday artistic vocabulary, and they came to him as naturally as they had to Tiepolo or Watteau or Cézanne or Picasso, as living and timeless poetic visual embodiments of a shared European artistic heritage, always available to symbolise the simultaneous fragility and joy of life. The many buxom maidens and musicians who populate his decorative universe were stock figures from within the traditions of European art, but they were also resolutely modern, and quite unlike the dreamy, if to our eyes now equally charming, knights in armour and damsels in distress of so much late Pre-Rapaelite decorative art that understandably seemed entirely inadequate in 1910 to express the urgent sense of a new and better age just around the corner.

As Vanessa's old friend, the French artist André Dunoyer de Segonzac wrote of her work some six months after her death in 1961,

The dominant characteristics of Vanessa's art are grandeur of conception, nobility and strength. (...) all is purity, frankness and perfect simplicity both in what is expressed and the means of expression. This accent of sincerity and truth has nothing to do with dull realism; it is stamped with a grand, natural distinction without a trace of affectation [...] "Fine painting" said Degas, "does not solicit"; and Vanessa succeeded in preserving throughout her life the sincerity and purity of her style. To these qualities she has added a discretion, reserve and modesty which remind us of the humility of a Cézanne or a Bonnard.[20]

Such a verdict would have moved her deeply, and is still valid today.

Neither Duncan Grant nor Vanessa Bell had initially encountered the work of Cézanne or Picasso and Matisse in a vacuum. On the contrary, they were both well-prepared for the encounter from their knowledge of the more abstract aspects of late-19th-century English art, such as the work of James Whistler, Edward Burne-Jones and Walter Crane. Like so many other young European artists, they responded above all to the thrilling potential of the new pictorial vocabulary emerging in Paris, which so precisely expressed their belief that a new world was dawning.

Yet in England, strangely, the work of the Bloomsbury artists is often dismissed in its entirety as merely derivative, especially by those who have rarely looked at it and who at the same time applaud the impact of Matisse and Picasso on artists in other countries. This is part and parcel of a long-standing tendency amongst English critics and art historians to assume that England is a country of little artistic significance compared to the nations of mainland Europe. This was an attitude that the artists of Bloomsbury came up against all their working lives and, sad to say, it has not gone away.

THE SUSSEX CONNECTION
THE PROSPECT OF ESCAPE

Towards the end of her long life Frances Partridge memorably observed that she sometimes thought, 'of the houses of geographical Bloomsbury as if they formed a key-ring from which hung a number of keys to other establishments'.[1] With incomparable skill she described the occupants of the various households of Gordon Square and the surrounding Georgian streets and adjacent squares in the 1920s, and the remarkable social and cultural life of that most creatively productive environment. That Bloomsbury is no more, save in legends and memoirs, the principal figures all being long dead, and their various London homes destroyed either by the Luftwaffe or by the equally implacable malice of the University of London in its ruthless redevelopment of the 1970s which resulted in so much needless damage to the area.

Bloomsbury, however, survives tenaciously as a state of mind, shared by many and expressed in a multitude of assumptions about the modern world, ranging from the role of women to the importance of the arts. It was such values that Bloomsbury promoted, and exported with them to Sussex. Already by 1900 the tentacles of Brighton had spread as far east as the formerly remote village of Telscombe and had all but engulfed the northerly villages of Patcham and Hangleton. Yet the broad stretch of countryside from Lewes to Eastbourne was still very much as it had been since the Norman conquest, especially along the northern escarpments of the South Downs.

Over a thousand years later, and presided over by the amiable genius of the Prince Regent, the transformation of the ancient fishing village of Brightelmstone into the chic resort of Brighton had made the Sussex coastline suddenly fashionable. In 1791 the new London-to-Brighton mail-coach took eight or nine hours to complete the journey, which was taken in long stages. By 1811, there were 28 coaches running daily, with the time cut to six hours.[2] Soon enough the railways followed.

Victoria Station in London's Pimlico district was incorporated in 1858 and initially divided into two halves, the east side serving the lines to Chatham and Dover, and the west side, finished in 1862, with its surviving grand hotel, serving Brighton and the Sussex coast. Both sections were largely rebuilt at the turn of the century, reflecting the age of glamorous steamer trains, including the romantically named Golden Arrow which linked London to Paris from 1929 until 1972.

In spite of all the many changes in recent years, on the right-hand side of the front entrance to the station there are still two large, delightful tile-maps of the southern railway network as it existed in around 1908 when the western façade of the station was rebuilt. Set well back in alcoves underneath the lettering of the Brighton and South Coast Railway Service, one shows the commuter lines to Surrey, with golf links and race courses prominently marked. The other extends to the sea, with further connections stretching all the way along the coastal strip from Hastings to the Isle of Wight, with special attention to castles and 'harbours for yachts', while at the bottom, a ferry steams its way jauntily out of Newhaven towards Dieppe. One was the prospect of stuffy suburbia, the other of escape.

William Blake and his wife lived for a few years at Felpham near Worthing around 1800, and various other artists and writers had briefly worked in or retired to Sussex in the course of the 19th century, including Sir Edward Burne-Jones who bought a house on the coast at Rottingdean in 1881, where he was frequently visited by William Morris. But no other creative group had come to Sussex in order to undertake their most important work, while never entirely renouncing their origins in the metropolis.

Roger Fry had built himself a substantial house just outside Guildford in 1908, but for most of Bloomsbury, Surrey represented the embodiment of just the kind of suffocatingly genteel late-Victorian suburban respectability which they most wanted to leave behind them. By contrast Sussex was still largely rural and remote working farm-land much as it had been since the gradual clearance of the ancient Wealden forests. Moreover, Fry's friends did not nurse similar architectural ambitions. Then, as now, Charleston at Firle and Monks House in Rodmell were approached by different railway lines running east from Lewes Station (mercifully spared the wholesale destruction of most Sussex railway stations in the 1970s). Charleston is most easily reached from Berwick station on the Brighton-Eastbourne and Hastings line, which runs several kilometres inland from the Downs and the village of Berwick, from which it takes its name. Leaving the train one follows the narrow road south, a risky task on foot these days but less dangerous than crossing the busy A27 road further on, in order either to follow the ancient bridleway along the foot of the Downs, or to cut across the fields. It was never a short walk. Rodmell was served by the Rodmell-Southease halt on the Seaford line which strikes south from Lewes across wide, flat watermeadows with gently rising hills on both sides.

Looking back at the end of his life, Leonard Woolf observed that

> The Leonard and Virginia Woolf who lived in Hogarth House, Richmond, from 1915 to 1924 were not the same people who lived in 52 Tavistock Square from 1924 to 1939; the Leonard and Virginia who lived in Asheham House from 1912 to 1919 were not the same people who lived in Monks House from 1919 to 1941. In each case the most powerful moulder of them and of their lives was the house in which they lived.[3]

Sadly the London flats and studios to which they and their friends' keyrings once gave access no longer exist, but with the exception of Asheham their homes in Sussex miraculously survive.

The connection between the Bloomsbury group and Sussex did not go unnoticed, Vanessa Bell was astonished to discover, writing to Roger Fry in 1927 concerning

*an extraordinary notice in the Westminster Gazette the other day headed
'Bloomsbury in Sussex', saying how the Woolves had their house and we and the
Keynes were near, how Duncan had a house in Gordon Sq. in which every inch
was of interest and had just taken on his villa at Cassis for 5 years, Mrs Bell had
3 children all gifted and good looking, gardens which she painted etc. etc. (...)
No one knows who wrote it.*[4]

She could not of course have imagined that so much of their work in London would later be destroyed, much of it not yet executed in 1927, and in this context the task of writing about Bloomsbury in Sussex takes on a rather different significance.

Both Vanessa and Virginia were strongly aware of the dangers involved in the inherited Victorian wifely role of 'angel in the house'. It is thus hardly surprising that they shared a strong ambivalence about home-making, albeit expressed in different ways. They had seen their mother sacrifice herself to the demands of child-rearing and the service of the household, and were determined not to repeat her story. It was this determination which propelled them into the invention of households which were without any precedent, but which in hindsight were intensely prophetic of wider social developments long after their own deaths. In their respective Sussex homes both sisters were able to turn their backs on the oppressive convention-bound social machinery of feminine decorum. In the following chapters I consider the environments they designed for themselves in which they explored their new and proudly proclaimed independence.

Note on spelling

There are variant spellings of Virginia Woolf's two Sussex homes. For the sake of clarity and consistency, I am using Asheham rather than Asham or Ascham, and Monks House, because that is the spelling that appears on the original deeds.

FIRLE & ASHEHAM

THE UTMOST QUIET AND REGULARITY

In January 1911 Virginia Stephen took possession of a newly-built gabled red-brick semi-detached house at the north end of the picturesque straggling village high street which runs through Firle, having taken on a lease in the previous month at the end of a year of nagging health problems. She was 29, and working on her first novel. A few kilometres east of Lewes at the foot of the Downs, Firle is a particularly charming village, though this could hardly be said of the house itself, a rather glum building which still looks oddly out of place in relation to its neighbouring cottages. Her description of it as a 'horrible suburban villa' rather suggests that she had second thoughts about it, but at a push it could sleep six people, and above all it was far away from all the hullabaloo of London, where she was currently living with her brother Adrian at 20 Fitzroy Square, at the start of her career as a professional writer.

Little Talland House

Its main significance lay simply in the fact that Virginia had found the confidence to take it on. Perhaps she was reacting to her older sister's six-year-old marriage which had left her somewhat stranded and cut off from Vanessa's stabilising motherly female influence, something for which she always looked throughout her life. Her thinking on the matter is most apparent from the name she gave it, Little Talland House, which brought together two important sets of personal associations.

Firstly, it summoned up a connection to Little Holland House in Kensington, the comfortable rambling home of her great-aunt Sara Prinsep and her husband Thoby, for whom, according to Virginia, her mother had cared more than for her own father.[1] Here the Prinseps had entertained many of the leading artists of the late 19th century including Burne-Jones, Holman Hunt, and especially G.F.Watts, together with leading contemporary scientists, writers and politicians, in a relaxed and eccentric style which in some ways anticipated that of their great-nieces.[2]

Still more significant was the association with Talland House, the substantial if rather shabby mid-Victorian villa looking out across the bay of St Ives in Cornwall where the Stephen family had taken regular family summer holidays between 1882 and 1894. Talland House provided Virginia with 'the most important of all my memories',[3] which shone all the brighter in contrast to the increasingly gloomy household to which they returned in Hyde Park Gate. Here she had been rapturously happy, an experience to which she repeatedly returned in her later fiction, most conspicuously in *To The Lighthouse* but also in the early sections of *The Waves*. Little Talland House was thus from the outset imagined as an opportunity to recreate something of the happily bohemian family life of the Prinseps, and the intense, idyllic joy she had experienced in Cornwall, with the implied suggestion that the pleasures of the past might be picked up again here, in a very different landscape.

From the start Vanessa helped her furnish it, but the house seems not to have quite taken off in the way Virginia must have hoped, though she spent many weeks alone there writing, and entertained numerous guests in the course of 1911. Of these much the most important was a visit in September by her friends Marjorie Strachey and Desmond MacCarthy, together with Leonard Woolf, a Cambridge friend of her late brother Thoby and of Lytton Strachey. Woolf had recently returned to London on leave from Ceylon (now Sri Lanka) where he had been working as a colonial administrator since 1904. It was on a typically bracing country walk with Leonard that Virginia first came across another empty house which was to play a major role in all their lives, and to which Little

Talland House must quickly have seemed merely a prelude. It was called Asheham House and the following month Virginia and Vanessa took out a joint one-year lease on it, allowing Robin Mayor, a civil servant and Fellow of King's College, Cambridge, to take up the tenancy of Little Talland House from Virginia a couple of months later.

This was a period of rapid change in Virginia's life, and only a month after taking on Asheham she and her younger brother Adrian moved out of 19 Fitzroy Square where they had separate flats, and into 38 Brunswick Square, together with Maynard Keynes and Duncan Grant, and from December, Leonard Woolf. Woolf quickly fell in love with her, and his courtship slowly prospered after numerous early rebuffs. In the following August they were married. A few months later they set up home in rented rooms in Clifford's Inn, right on the border of the City of London, which Virginia so loved, and there they began the task of home-making. However, by the summer of 1913 her mental health was rapidly deteriorating, and they moved out of central London to the quieter environment of Richmond. She was not to recover properly until late in 1915. It is against this background of marriage and long periods of severe illness requiring expensive nursing (at a time when they had almost no income) that the early years of life at Asheham need to be considered.

At this point it is helpful to say a few things about Leonard Woolf, whom Sir Geoffrey Keynes once described to me as the only saint he had ever met.[4]

Leonard Woolf

Leonard Woolf came from a large prosperous Jewish family, one of nine surviving children, who grew up in a large Kensington house, but were reduced to comparative poverty by his father's unexpected death when Leonard was a child, as a result of which the family was obliged to move to Putney. Later at Trinity College, Cambridge, he met Thoby Stephen, Lytton Strachey, Clive Bell and Saxon Sydney-Turner, and first saw Vanessa and Virginia in May 1900, when their beauty took his breath away. He did not show his feelings easily and Virginia's frank, spontaneous emotionalism expressed sentiments to which he himself could never adequately give public vent. As in so many relationships between fundamentally shy people, their intimacy is most clearly revealed in their many mutual nicknames, of which 'mongoose' and 'mandrill' are perhaps the most endearingly telling.

Pessimistic about human nature, Woolf was an ethical socialist and an equally ardent anti-imperialist, with no time for any theories based on notions of immutable laws, from Catholicism to Marxism. Rational, unillusioned, as hostile in his day to the unreflecting anti-Americanism of the New Statesman as to its equally naïve pro-Soviet and later pro-Maoist posturings, he was one of the first to denounce Hitler, and was appalled by the Labour Party's political prevarications in the 1930s. His spartan outlook admirably complemented his wife's essentially frugal style of home-life. By any standards they were both prodigious workers, he providing the perfect steady, reliable foil to her mercurial, capricious imagination. What she may have lacked in practical skills he made up for, just as she gave him access to a world of emotional spontaneity from which he was by temperament cut off. His five-volume autobiography is much the most important source of information about his wife, outside her own letters and diaries.

A man of rather narrow and at times puritanical rationality, he was entirely hostile to organised religion and social rituals rooted in snobbery and deference. Excessively fastidious, he was a compulsive list-maker, recording every last detail of their joint income and expenditure, and daily totting up the sum of the words he'd written, as well as jotting down almost everything that could be recorded, from his collection of gramophone records to the planting of his much-loved garden. Two years older than Virginia, he was above all a caring father-figure, but was also capable of mothering, and this must have been an important factor in her accepting him as her husband.

Unfortunately her mental health was into steady decline through the first half of 1913, leading to a major suicide attempt on 8 September, after which she was acutely ill for most of the next two years. In these frightening circumstances Sussex provided them both with space and time for stress-free work and everyday life, which proved a highly effective remedy until her final illness a quarter of a century later, brought on by the strain of the war and the devastation of her beloved London.

Asheham

In a talk given in 1931, Virginia Woolf explained that the novelist

> wants life to proceed with the utmost quiet and regularity. He wants to see the same faces, to read the same books, to do the same things day after day, month after month, while he is writing, so that nothing may disturb or disquiet the mysterious nosings about, feelings round, darts, dashes and sudden discoveries of that very shy and illusive spirit, the imagination.[5]

Thanks to Asheham this was precisely what she had finally found in Sussex. Asheham promised to be a place of recovery and it was here that she began to develop that strong sense of identification with the Sussex countryside which came to balance and complement her rich, historically informed sense of London. For the rest of their lives Leonard and Virginia would maintain homes in London and Sussex. Asheham gave her the possibility of a new equilibrium, while at the same time it was, as Richard Shone has noted, a 'rehearsal for both Monks House and Charleston'.[6]

Leonard Woolf left a description of how, on a walk from Firle whilst staying at Little Talland House, he and Virginia came across 'an extraordinarily romantic looking house', set 'in one of those lovely folds or hollows in the down'.[7] Set well back from the winding Lewes-Newhaven road behind a field full of sheep,

> It faced due west, and from its windows and terrace in front of the house you looked across the (…) Ouse valley to the line of the downs on the west of the river (…) There were barns behind the house, but there were no other buildings anywhere visible from it, indeed the only building anywhere near it was the shepherd's cottage. Its name was Asham house, sometimes written Asheham or Ascham.[8]

Built as a summer residence in the early 19th century by a Lewes solicitor, it was an extremely pretty Regency house with delightful twinned arched French windows along the front, which was flanked by two charming pedimented single-storey side pavilions. According to David Garnett the arched windows gave its façade 'a curiously dream-like character (...) not quite of the real world, like the houses in Walter De La Mare's novels'.[9] Inside there were two downstairs sitting-rooms, with four bedrooms above and a large attic. It still belonged to the original builder's grand-daughter, from whom Virginia obtained a five-year lease, and on 9 February, 1912 they gave a house-warming party attended by Vanessa Bell, Duncan Grant, Roger Fry, Clive Bell and Adrian Stephen.

Most of our information about life at Asheham comes from Virginia's letters, in which she rarely analysed her own feelings with any rigour, and in this context her descriptions of the house and surrounding landscape often seem to carry a metaphoric supplement suggestive of changing moods and states of mind. Indeed the Sussex landscape seems to have increasingly come to symbolise her inner self, reflected in the physical world to which she responded so urgently.

Largely written at Asheham, her first novel begins with a nocturnal journey down-river and away from the dangerous, glittering city of London, which only becomes glamorous as it recedes into darkness and memory. Published in 1915, *The Voyage Out* conducts its human cargo to a fabulous imaginary South America, where Rousseau-esque elephants and tigers creep out to pools under the cover of darkness and the coast-line sports an Elizabethan watch-tower, albeit ruinous. From the distance of the countryside she could shake off the pressures of London life, and something of her own sense of relief at getting away to Sussex is probably reflected on the part of her over-educated and emotionally fast-maturing young hero Terence, who muses:

> *Lord, how good it is to think of lanes, muddy lanes, with brambles and nettles, you know, and real grass fields, and farmyards with pigs and cows, and men walking beside carts with pitchforks – there's nothing to compare with that here – look at the stony red earth, and the bright blue sea, and the glaring white houses – how tired one gets of it!*[10]

Here she could also perhaps not resist taking a swipe at the associated Mediterranean world which was already so important to Vanessa. By contrast this was evidently a landscape that she had already come to know well for herself, under her own steam. Country walking had quickly become one of her greatest pleasures, partly for its own sake and partly to allow her to literally 'think out loud' about whatever she was writing or had on her mind. Local people thought Asheham haunted, and even Leonard Woolf, who was not in the least given to fantasy, wrote that he had never known a house 'which had such a strong character, personality of its own – romantic, gentle, melancholy, lovely'.[11] He also responded to the landscape of the South Downs, feeling from his first visits

> *the beauty of the gentle white curves of the fields between the great green curves of their hollows,* concluding that, *in all seasons and circumstances, their physical loveliness and serenity can make one's happiness exquisite and assuage one's misery.*[12]

The house was painted by Vanessa in a sequence of important pictures in 1912 in her most daringly modern stripped-down Post-Impressionist style. They show it very much as part of a working farm landscape with big haystacks nearby. There were several cottages in the vicinity housing tenant farm-workers and their families, from whom the Woolfs purchased local dairy produce and poultry directly. Sometimes they had to bicycle several kilometres for milk, on occasion as far as Glynde. In the early years Asheham was often rented out to close friends, including Maynard Keynes, and there were regular annual house-parties at Christmas and Easter.

Thanks to Leonard's impeccable book-keeping we know almost every last detail of their finances, a cautious reflection of his childhood reversals. At first, their annual income from Virginia's investments was under £400 a year, on top of which there was only a slender income from writing. With the cost of rent and Woolf's own meagre earnings they had just enough to survive.[13] There were to be no foreign holidays in the first ten years of their marriage. Her medical expenses were substantial and, in 1915, when his income from writing was less than £18, her medical bills amounted to no less than £500, obliging them to sell jewellery and securities in order to cover their costs.

The Hogarth Press, which they founded in 1917, earned them next to nothing in its first year and there were regular deficits in their joint income right up to 1923.[14] In time they were to become the first British publishers of Rilke, together with the work of a galaxy of other young talents, including their friend T.S. Eliot's *The Waste Land*, as well as writings by Gertrude Stein, Christopher Isherwood, Katherine Mansfield, Vita Sackville-West, Rebecca West, Rose Macaulay, and many others, besides Virginia's own books. Any early financial losses at the Press were more than compensated by its beneficial impact on Virginia's health, and the role it gave them together.

Meanwhile, down in Sussex, Mrs Funnell, the local shepherd's wife, came and 'did' for them, but by and large they looked after themselves. Leonard later recollected that 'our daily life was probably nearer Chaucer's than of the modern man, with water from the main, electricity, gas, cars, motor buses, telephone, wireless'.[15] All water had to be pumped from a well, and cooking was done on an oil stove or primus, with lighting by candles and oil lamps, and earth closets outside.

Sadly there is no proper photographic record of the interiors at Asheham, although there are several photos of its exterior, and of various friends on the terrace, including Vanessa painting a still-life on a table in front of her. Virginia had a complex relationship to home-making. She was intimidated to some extent by her older sister's remarkable domestic gifts, which she had the good sense to draw on but by which she did not want to be wholly swamped, while at the same time she was keen not to be sucked into the distracting demands of domesticity as an end in itself. Vanessa wrote to Virginia in August 1912 from Asheham where she was busy putting up curtains, having ordered 'a bright reddish orange stuff for curtains for the sitting room, to be lined and bordered with mauve'.[16] In 1914 Virginia attended cookery classes in Victoria Street, London, where she reported distinguishing herself 'by cooking my wedding ring into a suet pudding!'[17]

She was prone to be rather nervous about her own artistic judgement in the eyes of others, confiding to her diary in 1918 that she had been to the National Gallery with Roger Fry where she admired a Rembrandt which he thought melodramatic, whereas she found an Ingres 'repulsive' which was to him 'one of the most marvellous of designs', concluding – 'I always feel, too, that to like the wrong thing, or fail in sufficiently liking the right jars on him, like false notes, or sentimentality in writing'.[18] She was sometimes ill at ease at Charleston, feeling as out of her depth amongst artists as they did amongst her literary friends.

The early years at Asheham coincided with Duncan and Vanessa's involvement in the Omega Workshops in London, and much work for Omega was undertaken there, including the two panels of dancing figures which hung on the workshop façade.[19] In 1913 Vanessa and Duncan simultaneously painted portraits of Lytton Strachey seated outside on the back terrace against the flint garden wall; his version now hangs in the dining room at Charleston. Duncan Grant's *Abstract Kinetic Scroll* was also made here in 1914. Now in the collection of Tate Britain, it consists of a four-metre-long and partly collaged abstract painting, intended to be viewed through an aperture behind which it was moved between two rotating spindles, and it remains one of the most significant British contributions to experimental early Modernist art. At least one of the series of important portraits of Vanessa Bell in a red dress which he made in this period was also painted at Asheham. Visitors included Katherine Mansfield and E.M. Forster, and it was at Asheham that Carrington met Lytton Strachey for the first time in 1915. Vanessa and Duncan were less frequently there after the 1916 conscription crisis which led to the breakaway foundation of Charleston. Although Virginia rarely troubled to name the music she heard at concerts it is noteworthy that she recorded going to hear Debussy's new sonata for harp, flute and viola on 2 February 1917 in London, and it is music one may easily associate with the creative soul of the house.

From the outset Vanessa seems to have taken charge of the garden, which had lawns and flower-beds behind the terrace, and in September 1912 she had a large square flower-bed dug and planted. In April 1913

Virginia wrote to thank her for having planted the spring flowers outside 'which does you great credit' and to tell her that she and Leonard were putting in a rhodedendron hedge against one of the walls, which seems unlikely to have thrilled her.[20] In 1918 they planted red and yellow wall-flowers around the walled garden, with St John's Wort as ground-cover. There are also references to familiar cottage-garden flowers including primulas, sweet Williams, nasturtiums, columbines, peonies and dahlias, as well as Japanese anemones, of which Virginia was especially fond. There were also cooking-apples and plums, and she and Leonard frequently gathered wild mushrooms and blackberries which came in very useful during the food shortages in the final years of World War I. The sounds of coastal shelling were audible throughout the summer of 1918, just as 22 years later the windows at Monks House would rattle to the sound of bombs and anti-aircraft fire.

The Woolfs were not, however, to enjoy Asheham for long, since in 1918 they were given a year's notice, as it was required to house a gamekeeper. There was a farewell dinner party in August attended by Pernel Strachey (sister of Lytton), E.M. Forster, Vanessa Bell, Duncan Grant, Maynard Keynes, Roger Fry, Clive Bell and his mistress Mary Hutchinson. In 1927 major quarrying work began immediately behind the house for a new cement works which for more than 50 years was to belch dust across the entire valley below. The cement company purchased the house in 1932, and it stood for many years forlornly vacant and boarded up. In 1993 Lewes Council granted its new owners, the Blue Circle Waste Management, permission to extend its 12-year-old rubbish tip, subject to the resolution of the house's status as a listed building. In spite of its Grade II listing and a vigorous local campaign to save it, Asheham was finally bulldozed into oblivion on the 12 July 1994.

MONKS HOUSE

AN UNPRETENDING HOUSE

Perhaps reacting over-hastily to the loss of Asheham, in June 1919 Virginia impulsively bought the Round House in the middle of Lewes, the stump of a former windmill. However, only weeks later she discovered that a house she already knew in the nearby village of Rodmell was shortly coming on to the market. With a big garden to attract Leonard it was altogether a much better prospect, and she bought it at auction in July for £700, selling the newly purchased Lewes house two weeks later. Only referred to for the first time in documents as Monks House in 1919, it was, and remains, a small house, in spite of their later extensions.[1] It is, however, in an idyllic setting looking out across the water meadows of the Ouse valley with the Downs on both sides. Besides, Rodmell was a proper village, with its own pub and school and local traditions, and one senses that she preferred this to the bustle of Lewes or the isolation of Asheham and Vanessa's household out at Charleston. Vaughan-Williams had visited Rodmell in January 1906 where he listened to and transcribed the songs of local shepherds.

At the auction of its former contents the Woolfs bought various pieces of furniture, together with pots and pans and much gardening equipment. They also purchased three portraits of the Glazebrook family who had been former owners, and Leonard later recalled that he was deeply aware of the generations of previous occupants and that, as at Hogarth House in Richmond, he felt *a quiet continuity of people living. Unconsciously one was absorbed into this procession of men, women and children who since 1600 or 1700 (...) clattered up and down stairs, and had planted the great Blenheim apple-tree or the ancient fig-tree. One became a part of history and of a civilization by continuing in the line of all their lives.*[2]

Virginia let on to Saxon Sydney-Turner that she was at first finding it difficult to get over leaving Asheham 'though Leonard infinitely prefers this, chiefly on account of the garden, which pours pears and plums and apples and vegetables upon us' while she preferred the views of the Downs across the water meadows.[3] Monks House was also in a badly neglected condition throughout, and although, as she informed Lytton Strachey, she at first found it 'very humble and unromantic compared with Asheham' there was the consolation of 'the morning sun in one's window'.[4] By September she confided in her diary that she considered Monks House much improved 'after the fashion of a mongrel who wins your heart'.[5]

It was, as she at once perceived,

an unpretending house, long & low, a house of many doors; on one side fronting the street of Rodmell, & wood boarded on that side, though the street of Rodmell is at our end little more than a cart track running out on to the flat of the water meadows.[6]

Writing many years later her niece Angelica Garnett recalled that the house

was long and narrow: The rooms opened out of each other in succession, the whole house lower than the garden outside, so that one stepped into it rather as one steps into a boat. Plants and creepers knocked at the small-paned windows as though longing to come in, invited perhaps by the green walls (...) Green was Virginia's colour; a green crystal pear stood always on the table in the sitting-room, symbol of her personality.[7]

Internally Monks House feels oddly disconnected, the more so due to the various higgledy-piggledy additions over the years, involving several half-staircases to rooms at bewilderingly different levels. The front and back, moreover, seem to relate to one another in only the most provisional of ways, and going from photographs one would not necessarily guess that they belonged to one and the same house. With no electricity, mains water or drains, it was cold, damp and primitive, and they began at once to rebuild and improve the kitchen, adding a solid-fuel oven in 1920. The kitchen was further improved by a local Lewes firm in 1926 together with the provision of instant hot water and a bathroom above the kitchen, in which Virginia could enjoy the luxury of a bath every morning after breakfast. Many years later their housekeeper Louie Mayer recalled often hearing her rehearsing out loud in the bath the fictional dialogue that she'd composed in the night, just like Charles Dickens.[8] As at Asheham, Virginia and Leonard had separate bedrooms.

Virginia reported regularly to Vanessa about her ongoing decoration of the house, and asked questions about how to mix paint and so on. By 1926 she privately thought Monks House

> a perfect triumph (...) In particular our large combined drawing eating room, with its 5 windows, its beams down the middle, & flowers & leaves nodding in all round us. The bath boils quickly; the water closets gush & surge (not quite sufficiently though).[9]

Vanessa, however, continued to compare it unfavourably to Charleston. A critical visit in August 1922 left Virginia asking herself, with some evident annoyance, why she shouldn't stand up for herself, 'and defy them, even in the matter of hats and chair covers?'[10] Her anxieties and inhibitions in this area were not unlike those affecting her wider experience of shopping, especially for clothes, about which she was always painfully self-conscious. As she observed in *Orlando*, our clothes have 'more important offices than merely to keep us warm. They change our view of the world and the world's view of us'.[11]

It was this latter view to which she was particularly sensitive, just as she disliked being drawn or painted or having her photograph taken. Her inability to trust her own artistic judgement had its longstanding counterpart in Vanessa's much protested inability to write. This was all part of their mutual fiction about one another, developed in their adolescence — a view that was never, at any time in their lives, to prove susceptible of revision on the part of either sister.

Home-making could be a torture for her, and she wrote tellingly to Vita Sackville-West in 1926 of her dislike of shopping induced by

> *a torrent of duties (...) you can't think how many mattresses and blankets new sheets pillowcases, petticoats and dustpans I haven't had to buy. People say one can run out to Heals and buy a mattress: I tell you it ruins a day; 2 days: 3 days — Every time I get inside a shop all the dust in my soul rises, and how can I write next day? Moreover, somehow my incompetence, and shopkeepers not believing in me, harasses me into a nagging harpy.*[12]

Vita was evidently one of the few people in whom she could confide about such anxieties.

Meanwhile, Virginia got on with the task of decorating the house, leaving the garden to Leonard. At the end of February 1920 she painted the dining room a pomegranate colour and reported in a letter to Lady Robert Cecil that she was 'splashing red and yellow paint everywhere'.[13] Six years later she wrote to Vanessa asking her advice about curtains and chair covers for the drawing rooms and asking her to paint the exposed beams, which seems not to have happened. She also asked rather sheepishly if she might

> *be allowed some rather garish but vibrating and radiating green and red lustres on the mantelpiece? Showers of glass, shaped like long fingers in a bunch — you know my taste that way. Also I want to buy a ship in a glass bottle: also a mother of pearl and wooden platter. But I will wait for you.*[14]

In 1927 she was painting another room blue, and wrote instructing Vanessa only half mock-complainingly:

> *For Gods sake take up the making of wallpapers. I'm sick of the long monotony of distemper, besides which, when dry it is totally different from what one expects.*[15]

She evidently didn't try making sample strips.

Home improvements

Virginia completed her first two novels at Asheham, and the process of settling down more permanently at Monks House was the precondition for the great sequence of books which was to follow, alongside prodigious quantities of occasional writings in the form of short stories, reviews and essays. She finished *Jacob's Room* in November 1921 and was working on *Mrs Dalloway* from 1922 until 1924, followed by *To The Lighthouse*, which was published in 1927, and *Orlando* in 1928.

The pattern of rebuilding and furnishing increasingly followed the sales of her books, especially as she became more successful. A new oil stove was delivered in September 1925 which revolutionised the kitchen, on the same day that work began on a new greenhouse. In February 1927 she proudly informed Vita Sackville-West that they had two lavatories installed, 'one paid for by Mrs Dalloway, the other by The Common Reader'.[16] Until then, they had been using an outside earth closet.

She was moreover justifiably proud of her new income, confiding to her diary in 1929 that 'For the first time we have made over £400 profit. I think with pride that 7 people depend, largely, upon my handwriting on a sheet of paper (. . .). It's not scribbling, it's keeping 7 people fed and housed.'[17] Electricity arrived in 1931, together with a refrigerator, and electric fires in all the bedrooms and lighting throughout. The house was connected to the water mains in 1934. A two-storey extension was added in 1930 providing her with her own small upstairs sitting-room in which she appears in many photographs, above a bedroom entered from the garden. In the winter of 1934 she had a new free-standing wooden studio built away from the house at the churchyard end of the garden on the site of an earlier studio, with windows on both sides and glazed double-doors looking across to Mount Caburn. This was her 'lodge', in which she wrote in the summer months, and from which she reported in the hot August of 1937 that the Downs appeared 'the colour of lions'.[18] The telephone (Lewes 385) was installed in January 1932.

At Monks House Virginia was always keen to assert something of herself alongside the prevailing Bloomsbury decor, much of which we see today. Besides buying new furniture in London, including beds from

Heal's in 1931, when her new ground-floor bedroom was ready, she also picked up crockery and the odd bit of furniture on holiday in France. In 1928 she had purchased a comfortable sofa, out of pity for her friends, she claimed to Vanessa.[19] Although in the early years there was little room for overnight guests, she was much more gregarious than Vanessa, and there was a constant stream of visitors who sometimes subsequently complained to one another about the cold, or having felt neglected. T.S. Eliot was a fairly frequent visitor to both Rodmell and Richmond in the early 1920s. On one visit E. M. Forster famously singed his trousers warming himself against a Cosy-Stove.

Many things were commissioned directly from Vanessa and Duncan, including the table and monogrammed chairs now in the sitting room, which were ordered in 1929. Virginia bought three painted trays from Vanessa in December 1929, two of which are still in the house, and in April 1929 she wrote to her to order new plates, a green bowl and a small lampshade.[20] She also purchased a desk and more furniture by Duncan and Vanessa in late 1932 from the ideal Music Room they exhibited at the Lefevre Gallery.[21] These included the small upright cupboard with a mirrored recess now in the Dining Room at Monks House. She bought a three-panel screen by Vanessa too (no longer in the house) with three seated female figures, two of whom carry musical instruments, and are sisters to the slightly earlier seated maidens from Duncan's sitting-room fireplace at Charleston. Virginia's tastes are revealed in a letter to Duncan Grant thanking him for the arrival of a new carpet she had commissioned from him for 52 Tavistock Square:

> as you know, it is the dream of my life to be a tropical fish swimming in a submerged forest; and now that is permanently gratified – with what effect on my morals, my art, my religion, my politics, my whole attitude to reality, God only knows . . . .[22]

A table decorated by Duncan arrived just after Christmas 1930, and she bought another table from Vanessa in 1931, commissioning her at the same time to undertake a tiled fireplace for her new upstairs sitting-room, sending her the measurements in July.[23] In September she wrote, rather ungraciously, to tell Vanessa she was 'getting attached' to it but thought that 'perhaps the proportions are wrong'.[24] She was however entranced by the embroidery-framed mirror for the sitting room designed by Duncan and worked by his mother Ethel, which arrived for Christmas 1937 and is still at Monks House.[25] She wrote again to thank Mrs Grant for a second mirror in August 1938. One of the final changes involved the conversion of a long attic space into a library for Leonard, together with a tiled fireplace by Duncan Grant which is still *in situ*.

Virginia walked a great deal, often with Leonard, and the routine of Sussex life provided an important calming backdrop to her major work between the wars. They were constantly making discoveries, including Amberley near Chichester, and places nearer home such as East Chiltington which, she informed the staunchly Francophile Vanessa rather cattily, 'in its way beats St Remi, to say nothing of Cassis – only 3 miles the other side of Lewes'.[26] Travel was made easier by the purchase of a second-hand Singer car in 1927, which they replaced with a new coffee-and-chocolate-coloured car with a roll-back top in February 1929. This was also a Singer. As in his dealings with electrical equipment, Leonard evidently liked to stick with what he knew.

The Woolfs spent about one fifth of their time in Sussex in the 1920s, rising to a third by the early 1930s. As Vanessa's daughter Angelica observed, their relationship was

> *above all comradely: deeply affectionate and indivisibly united, they depended on each other. They knew each other's minds and therefore took each other for granted – they accepted each other's peculiarities and shortcomings and pretended no more than they could help.*[27]

Leonard's life had changed in 1923 when he was appointed as the literary editor of the *Nation*, for which he earned £500 a year, an enormous help to their joint finances, and a job he maintained until 1930 when the income from the Hogarth Press and from Virginia's books began to kick in. In 1929 her annual royalties had risen to nearly £3,000 following the success of *To The Lighthouse* and *Orlando,* and at the age of 49 Leonard gave up regular employment in order to concentrate on the

Hogarth Press, while they spent increasing amounts of time in Rodmell.[28] In his autobiography he provides a self-revealingly concise summary of their earnings for the years 1924-1939.[29]

On most days they worked separately in the mornings, and after lunch he gardened whilst she relaxed or went walking. She mainly wrote at a very low armchair with a plywood board across her knees, with an inkstand glued to it. Always extremely fastidious about ink and pens and nibs, she wrote on notebooks of plain paper which she often covered in coloured paper. Later in the day she would type up the morning's work, revising as she went. Tirelessly productive, she was, as Hermione Lee points out, very far from being 'the delicate lady authoress of a few experimental novels and sketches' but was rather 'one of the most professional, perfectionist, energetic, courageous and committed writers in the language'.[30]

Home life

Virginia's homes were to differ as far as possible from the theatres of conspicuous domestic self-sacrifice and feminine wiles which she associated in her writings with the person of 'The Angel in the House', of whom her mother had been such a terrible example, dead before she was 50, a mother of seven and worn away by good deeds and purity. Her former cook and housekeeper Louie Mayer left a fascinating account of life at Monks House where she worked for 34 years, having initially answered an advertisement which the Woolfs had placed in a local newspaper in the summer of 1934. She was thrilled to get the job at a time when 'seven shillings and sixpence a week and a cottage rent-free was really a big wage'.[31] Both Leonard and Virginia she recalled 'went to a lot of trouble to make me feel at home and help me adjust to their routine. I liked them both the very first week.' He made the coffee at eight o'clock every morning and took it out to Virginia's bedroom, entered from the garden, where she 'had always been working during the night'. Incidentally providing fascinating glimpses of different house-guests, she described the touching scene of Virginia turning up at her cottage to let her know that she'd finished *The Years*, and telling her she was going to get the kitchen repainted and 'lots of new things put in for you. She was so excited that we spent the rest of the afternoon making plans'.[32] She was seemingly the last person to see Virginia alive, and stayed on until Leonard's death.

Although not much of a cook, Virginia particularly liked baking bread. She could also be endearingly childish in the kitchen, shaping a pastry dog's head – the colophon of the Hogarth Press – to go on the lid of a plum tart in 1925.[33] Angelica Garnett recalls that she could also bottle fruit, and took pride 'in her cupboard of jade-green gooseberries and sad-purple raspberries on the stairs at Monks House'.[34] A home, an office and a place of work, and never conventionally comfortable, it was a house of 'ramshackle informality' as Leonard put it.[35] They lived frugally, spending little on clothes or luxuries. They bought books but were not serious collectors and were both subscribers to the London Library. Virginia worked periodically on embroidery which she claimed to Vanessa, from whom she commissioned designs, to find 'soothing'.[36] At the end of her life she also worked to designs by Angelica.

She and Leonard played countless games of bowls with one another as well as family and friends on the back lawn outside, and they kept a succession of dogs and other pets, of which his much-loved marmoset Mitz was the most demanding, since she had to be kept indoors or she would disappear up trees from which she could only be lured down by honey. She also had a passion for macaroons and tapioca pudding, which must say something about the cuisine at Monks House. There was later a cat. Virginia shopped in Lewes but also sometimes ordered food by post from London including delicacies such as macaroni which was not to be had locally in 1939. There are gossipy references throughout her diary to local events, local weather, and local people, suggesting a growing sense of belonging, always balanced by her love of seclusion.

Music

As a young woman Virginia had been a keen concert and opera-goer, though she seemed more interested in the audience than details of production or performance. She and Leonard listened a great deal to broadcast radio concerts and the gramophone. In the 1920s he had been a member of the National Gramophone Society, from which he resigned in 1926 in protest at the quality of a recording of Schubert's string quintet. After World War II he was for some years a member of The Record Society, and subsequently bought a tape-recorder to record broadcast concerts. They both evidently admired the pianist Arthur Schnabel, as well as the Busch Quartet whom they went out of their way to hear perform in London. Their E.M.G. Handmade Gramophone Company gramophone and wireless is still at Monks House, and for many years Leonard bought records directly from the company, especially works by Bach, Beethoven and Mozart.[37]

In the library of the University of Sussex is a collection of tiny hand-written cards recording the dates and details of the records he played, which reveal much about his musical tastes. They include Beethoven's quartets, the symphonies, piano and chamber music of Haydn and Schubert, Mozart's trios and piano concertos, and Bach's chamber music which he evidently knew extremely well, including not only the celebrated cello and violin sonatas but also work for the viola da gamba, as well as all the keyboard music. In later life he kept up with new performers including Glenn Gould, Sviatoslav Richter, and the Amadeus Quartet, as well as returning to pre-war favourites such as the Busch, Budapest, Hungarian, Pascal and Pro Arte Quartets. He also much admired soloists including Casals, Solomon, and Landowska, of whose harpsicord recording of the Goldberg Variations he was evidently especially fond. In the 1950s he often listened to Victoria de los Angeles singing Spanish songs, reflecting a sunnier side of his temperament than is sometimes apparent.[38]

A notebook in Leonard's shaky handwriting also records the broadcast music to which he listened almost daily from 1939 to 1968, not infrequently making excursions outside his usual listening habits, including several broadcast operas in 1939: Verdi's *La Traviata* (31 May) and *Macbeth* (7 July), both on the BBC, as well as Donizetti's *Don Pasquale* from Rome on 19 March, suggesting Virginia's hand on the tuning dial in the days when one could listen in to regular classical broadcasts from Brussels, Cologne, Hilversum, Lille, Paris, Strasburg and so on.[39]

The war

By October 1938 there were sandbags piled up around Bloomsbury against the threat of war. In August the Woolfs moved out of 52 Tavistock Square, where they had lived since leaving Hogarth House in 1924, taking on a flat at 37 Mecklenburgh Square in the first week of the war. The rise of the dictators and rumours of war occur increasingly throughout Virginia's diaries from the mid-1930s, and they shared their friends' sense of helpless hopelessness in the face of the inability of the political leadership of Britain and France to offer any resistance. They were back in Rodmell on 3 September when war was finally declared.

It is perhaps easy to forget how close to the edge of catastrophe things felt in England prior to and after the fall of France. On 14 June 1940, on a day out with Vita Sackville-West, Virginia visited Penshurst Place, the ancestral home of Sir Philip Sidney, as the Germans marched into Paris. She and Leonard still made regular visits to London before the Blitz began in June 1940, but she spent most of her time at Rodmell, working on her life of Roger Fry and her final novel, *Between The Acts*. This was largely inspired by an invitation in April 1940 from the Women's Institute in Rodmell to write and produce a village play, for which she eventually lent her kitchen table in August.[40] In the event, an air-raid siren sounded in the middle of the performance and was completely ignored, to her great admiration.[41] Back from London at the end of June 1940, she exclaimed to her diary:

> *Three solitary nights. Think of that! Was there ever such a miracle? Not a voice, not a telephone. Only the owl calling; perhaps a clap of thunder, the horses going down to the Brooks, & Mr Botten [farmer] calling with the milk in the morning.*[42]

One afternoon, however, in August 1940, they had to fling themselves down on the ground outside in the garden, hands behind their heads, as German planes flew low overhead and bombs shook the windows of her writing lodge.[43] Her diaries from this time marvellously capture the unreality and even the beauty of war: 'Duncan saw an air battle over Charleston – a silver pencil and a puff of smoke'.[44]

Their former home at Tavistock Square was completely destroyed by enemy action in October 1940, and Virginia wrote to Edward Sackville-West describing how she had seen the drawing-room panels painted by Vanessa and Duncan 'suspended over the rubble'.[45] Mecklenburgh Square was made uninhabitable on 9 September. Virginia managed to recover various belongings from the downstairs tenants, although she was at times quite exhilarated at the prospect of shedding possessions. Leonard was able to transfer the operations of the Hogarth Press to Letchworth in Hertfordshire, where many of its books were printed. He also managed to organise the transfer of many of their belongings into a couple of spare rooms in a Rodmell farmhouse – until the owner changed his mind, fearing they might be a fire-hazard if hit by a bomb – while their many now-damp books were deposited in a former shop.

Virginia's letters and diaries contain memorable descriptions of the blitzed streets of London, and she reported sadly to Vita in January 1941 'All my lovely squares gone'.[46] Yet as she explained to Ethel Smyth, with a typically brilliant metaphor, 'I try to let down a fire-proof curtain and go on reading, writing, cooking'.[47] She wrote to Vanessa of her admiration for Winston Churchill and

> *the tweed wearing sterling dull women here, with their grim good sense: organising First aid, putting out bombs for practice, and jumping out of windows to show us how.*[48]

She also possessed a certain gift for making virtues out of necessity, as when a stray bomb burst the river-bank flooding the adjacent water-meadows, which immediately inspired her to invite Vita over:

> *Not to see me. To see the flood. A bomb burst the banks. We are so lovely – all sea, right up to the gate. I've never seen anything more visionary lovely than Caburn upside down in the water. Flocks of gulls. Do come at once, Oh and a boat: and haystacks in the flood.*[49]

She finished the first draft of *Between The Acts* in November 1940, about which she recorded feeling 'a little triumphant'.[50] Set in a fictionalised Rodmell transported to the Midlands, it centres on the production of a village pageant, now all too rare but still common in my childhood in the 1960s. The history of England is enacted by villagers who were being rapidly squeezed off the land as technology devoured the need for manpower, so much so that by the 1940s Rodmell had lost half the former 160 inhabitants it had been home to 35 years previously.[51] She and Leonard were by now effectively cut off in Rodmell, yet like most people they were resilient in the face of adversity, and Virginia – now making her own butter and breakfasting off home-pickled eggs – described rationing and shortages as 'inconveniences rather than hardships'.[52] The last words in her diary for 1940 dryly note 'How one enjoys food now: I make up imaginary meals'.[53]

By August 1940 German planes had long been screaming overhead, sometimes firing arbitrarily into the village and threatening death at any moment, about which she was decidedly sanguine. But she was haunted by the devastation of London, a city she loved with the most intensely physical as well as visionary passion. By 1941, she realised she was again beginning to lose her mind, and not wanting to put her loved ones through the hell of caring for her in such terrible circumstances, on 28 March she drowned herself in the nearby Ouse. The previous evening Leonard recorded their listening to Beethoven's Appassionata sonata on the radio. As Hermione Lee puts it so well,

> Virginia Woolf was a sane woman who had an illness. She was often a patient, but she was not a victim. She was not weak, or hysterical, or self-deluding, or guilty, or oppressed. On the contrary, she was a person of exceptional courage, intelligence and stoicism, who made the best use she could, and came to the deepest understanding possible to her, of her own condition. She endured, periodically, great agony of mind and severe physical pain, with remarkably little self-pity.[54]

Emphasising her great capacity for joy, the novelist Elizabeth Bowen described their last meetings at Rodmell during the war as they together hemmed a torn curtain in the house 'and she sat back on her heels and put her head back (. . .) and laughed in this consuming, choking, delightful, hooting way'.[55]

Leonard buried her ashes under a tall elm overlooking the meadows, one of two trees they had nicknamed after themselves. The tree fell in 1943.

Afterlife

Picking up his life again, in 1943 Leonard took a lease at 24 Victoria Square, where he got to know the publisher Ian Parsons and his artist wife Trekkie as near neighbours. He continued to travel regularly to London on Labour Party and Hogarth Press business, living long enough to see the latter's 50th anniversary in 1967, by which time it was a successful subsidiary of Chatto & Windus. He continued to garden, travel and write, and found personal happiness in his close friendship with Trekkie Parsons, to whom he left Monks House, because he did not want it to become a 'literary shrine'.

In Rodmell he served as Clerk of the Parish Council for 17 years, and was much detained with parish business, from vandalism to the repair of walls and the maintenance of public rights of way. For many years he was treasurer of the local cricket club, a manager of the local primary school, and president of the local horticultural society. Louie Mayer later recalled that

> *Mr Woolf was so active, he almost ran everywhere as though he needed more hours in the day, and he worked hard all the time. He really could work. He was also a very kind and thoughtful man. When I was ill a few years ago, and had to have an operation, he came every day to the hospital in Brighton to talk to me (...) When Mr Woolf died my work at Monk's house came to an end. I had been there for thirty-six years. They were very happy years, I had loved my work, and become very fond of Mr and Mrs Woolf. I was always glad I had noticed that advertisement in the local newspaper in Southease all that time ago, and had answered it.* [56]

Peggy Ashcroft read Milton's *Lycidas* at his cremation. The elm in the garden beneath which his ashes were buried fell victim to Dutch elm disease in 1985. Monks House passed in time to the University of Sussex, and is now cared for by The National Trust.

At the end of *Orlando* Virginia Woolf describes its centuries-old owner returning home to the great house based on Knole in Kent, where

> she fancied that the rooms brightened as she came in; stirred, opened their eyes as if they had been dozing in her absence (...) as if so long a life as theirs had stored in them a myriad moods which changed with winter and summer, bright weather and dark, and her own fortunes and the people's characters who visited them. Polite, they always were to strangers, but a little weary; with her, they were entirely open and at their ease.[57] There were however everywhere *little lavender bags to keep the moth out and printed notices, 'Please do not touch', which, though she had put them there herself, seemed to rebuke her. The house was no longer hers entirely, she sighed. It belonged to time now; to history; was past the touch and control of the living (...) Chairs and beds were empty (...) The great wings of silence beat up and down the empty house.*[58]

For all the differences between Monks House and the vast rambling town-like Knole, we may be forgiven similar feelings at Rodmell, in a place so similarly charged and impressed with its makers' presence.

Monks House today

In spite of the various extensions made to it over the years, Monks House is not large, and in a way the old-fashioned bathroom with its downwards tilting bath is as telling as anything of the place. The Woolf's set of bowls still sit in an old wooden crate under the stairs, and Virginia's standard white enamel bread bin is just visible in the kitchen. The big downstairs sitting-room which they had opened up by removing internal partitions has been repainted a gloopy modern apple-green, somewhat darker than the paint exposed above the back door into the conservatory, which is closer to eau-de-nil.

Of its original furnishings it still contains Duncan's embroidered upright fire-screen with his signature white vase, and an exceptionally beautiful 1930 tile-topped table decorated by Duncan with two semi-clad goddesses flanked by little boats at sea. Leonard's old radio-gramophone stands at the far end, with one big cabinet-sized corner speaker. A stylishly modern 1930s bentwood armchair has a companion out in Virginia's lodge. Another she gave to Vanessa, now at Charleston, the pond of which appears on one wall in a nice 1934 watercolour by Vanessa. Other paintings include two still-lives by Vanessa, and a beautiful 1936 view of Newhaven Harbour, done on one of her regular painting trips out in the car with Duncan.

The three 19th-century Glazebrook family pictures are still in the house, including the strange painting, now in the kitchen, of a man with a horse and a little girl with a dog beside a canal in a dream-like industrial urban landscape. Against the opposite wall stands a glazed wooden cabinet, now stripped of its former green paint, but still housing a nice display of Bloomsbury ceramics including a small dark blue Omega Workshops plate, several octagonal plates richly decorated with classical goddesses, and several pieces of Vanessa's 1934 blue-and-white Bizarre dinner service designed for Clarice Cliff. In this of all houses they perfectly complement Vanessa's dust-jackets for her sister's books.

The dining room is really no more than a recess from the central corridor which runs along the back of the house and was never capable of any sense of enclosure. The cane-backed chairs were bought from Vanessa and Duncan's 1932 Music Room exhibition, as was the small mushroom-coloured cabinet. Above the undecorated wooden fireplace hangs another Glazebrook family group, opposite a particularly beautiful 1917 still-life of apples on a plate by Vanessa. It is a very close relation to a painting by Duncan, now in Sydney, Australia, which was doubtless painted at the same time, like several other pictures in this period, including the two 1914 versions of the *Mantelpiece Still-Life* in the collection of Tate.[59] Just around the corner in the hall is an embroidery-framed mirror designed by Duncan and described by Virginia as 'the loveliest looking glass I've ever seen'.[60] It also has a sister at Charleston, and they quietly and endlessly evoke one another. Virginia's own face appears on the other side of the hall in Vanessa's haunting 1912 portrait.

Nothing remains from his time in Leonard's former attic study except for a solitary low cane-backed armchair, often seen around the house in old photographs and no longer in the best state of repair, and Duncan's blue-and-turquoise tiled fireplace with its huge bouquet of flowers at the top. This makes for instructive comparison with Vanessa's 1931-32 tiled fireplace in Virginia's upstairs sitting-room, with its big Madonna lilies on the sides, which must originally have had a small frontal hearth-section, of which two fragments survive surrounded now by badly damaged, rather nasty imitation Dutch 17th-century replacements. Best of all however is Vanessa's 1930 tiled fireplace in Virginia's ground-floor bedroom, with its central oval cartouche of a yacht and lighthouse, and its delicate green pilasters together with Vanessa's autograph sun-disk motif, here painted blue.

The garden

In later years Trekkie Parsons enlarged Virginia's 'lodge', the former space now visible from the side windows and through a dark modern glass wall – not really a very satisfactory situation. It houses a big table with a few writing things on it, too few really to suggest her personality. According to Leonard it was here that she wrote her suicide note in March 1941.

Initially both Leonard and Virginia were involved in plans for the garden but it soon became his domain, just as the interior decorating was hers. It was a large walled garden behind the house, including two ponds and a croquet lawn, together with an orchard and large vegetable patch beyond, and an adjacent meadow purchased in 1928 to prevent its being built on.

Nigel Nicolson thought that although his mother Vita had nothing to do with the garden at Charleston, she attempted to have her say at Monks House, but 'not with great success, because she never ceased to despair about the lack of visual taste in either of the Woolves'.[61] If so, this was rather unfair of her, since Leonard went in for effective bold plantings with masses of traditional cottage-garden flowers such as asters, zinnias, nasturtiums, dahlias, irises and so on, as well as growing and tending orchids and other exotics in the greenhouse, doubtless reminding him of his years in Ceylon.

Much of the garden statuary came from the unlikely source of a grocer's shop in Crawley, as Virginia reported in 1937, *where Leonard is going to buy a leaden Cupid for his new water garden. He has a passion for ponds; and whenever the grocer has a cupid to sell, we buy it, to stand naked, with a tortoise balanced on the bow.* [62]

This was perhaps the origin of the cast of Donatello's David from the Bargello Museum in Florence, now in the back greenhouse, which formerly overlooked a raised oval pool edged with egg-and-dart decoration. One recalls that there was a plaster cast of a Roman statue of Antinous, the favourite of the Emperor Hadrian, which stood for many years on the far side of the pond at Charleston, until it eventually fell victim to frost in 1954. The final poignant words of her diary are 'L. is doing the rhododendrons'. [63]

Getting there National grid ref. TQ421063

- Monks House is open to visitors from Easter to late October on Wednesday and Saturday afternoons. It is necessary to book in advance.
- **Website:** www.nationaltrust.org.uk
- **Telephone enquiries:** 01323 870001.
- **By road:** Monks House is signposted to the left of the A26 Lewes to Newhaven road at Rodmell, beside the Abergavenny Arms.
- **Cycling:** View the National Cycle Network website: www.sustrans.org.uk
- **By rail:** The nearest railway station is Southease on the Lewes/Newhaven line, which is 1 mile (2 kilometres) away from Rodmell. For train times phone the national enquiry line: 08457 484950.
- **By bus:** The 123 service runs between Lewes bus station and Firle. Call Traveline for the times of services: 0870 608 2608 or visit their website: www.travelinesoutheast.org.uk

CHARLESTON

MOST LOVELY, VERY SOLID AND SIMPLE

Charleston is a large, solid, open-faced farm-house built of local flint and brick around an older timber-framed core in the high farming days of the 18th century to serve the fertile land along the northern escarpment of the South Downs between Glynde and Firle. Still surrounded by working farm buildings, it has some 14 rooms arranged on two floors, with attics and out-buildings. Its solitude was formerly more softened by a surrounding screen of trees, most of which sadly fell victims to Dutch elm disease and the great storm of 1987.

The circumstances surrounding Vanessa Bell's renting of Charleston in 1916 have been frequently described. She had recently ended an affair with Roger Fry and fallen in love with her longstanding colleague Duncan Grant, who faced imminent conscription to serve in a war of which he and all his friends disapproved. Stepping in to take charge of the situation after his military tribunal she found herself urgently needing somewhere to house herself, together with her two young sons, as well as Duncan and his fellow conscientious-objector and friend David Garnett, both of whom were required to work on the land as a condition of their exemption from military service. Having been alerted to the availability of the house by her sister earlier in the year she now moved swiftly, taking out her first tenancy agreement in a matter of weeks. Her permanent home between 1916 and 1919, Charleston was subsequently used as a holiday home for the next two decades, though she and Duncan might spend anything up to three or four months there in the course of any given year. Life was rough and ramshackle, and electricity did not arrive until 1933.

Shortly before the outbreak of World War II they decided to move permanently to Sussex, largely in response to the death, in 1937, of Vanessa's much-loved older son Julian, while serving as an ambulance driver in the Spanish Civil War, from which she never fully recovered. In 1939 they fortunately moved down some, though by no means all, of their London possessions, the rest of which perished together with their studios in 1940. Charleston remained their main home for the rest of their lives, though they maintained a sequence of small London studio flats after the war. From the outset it is important to note that Duncan and Vanessa never owned Charleston; they rented it from the Gage family to whom it had belonged since time out of mind. By the time of Duncan's death in 1978, the whole place was in a badly run-down state, and its future was, to say the least, uncertain. Quentin Bell feared that all that could be done was to salvage the removable painted doors and panels and offer them to the Victoria & Albert Museum.[1]

Happily fate intervened in the capable person of Deborah Gage, who inspired the formation of a Trust in 1980 which successfully raised sufficient funds to purchase the lease and to undertake a thorough and exemplary restoration of the house and garden, which opened to the public in June 1986. Although this would doubtless have surprised its former occupants, they would, I think, have been pleased, albeit in their characteristically modest and self-deprecating manner. Though purged of much of its former clutter, Charleston remains unnervingly like the home it was for some 60 years, shabbily comfortable, and decorated throughout in a style which hauntingly evokes the skills and values of the people who lived there. The Rouaults may be gone from the dining room and the Picasso and tiny early Matisse from the sitting room, but there are still many drawings and other works of art on display which remind us of the remarkable creative dialogue between England and France in the early decades of the last century, of which Vanessa Bell and Duncan Grant were such leading exponents.

At Charleston they produced an endless stream of designs and paintings representing a faith in modern art which had little institutional support in England. Asserting their role as artists within the wider field of interior decoration, they created total environments which became, in effect, works of art in their own right, while also functioning as fully working homes in which their pictures could be seen to the best advantage, and where the claims and implications of a wholly new personal lifestyle could be explored.

To some extent they were successors to the decorators of the Arts and Crafts movement, not least in their liking for embroidery and screens, but with a much stronger emphasis on the direct trace of the artist's hand, and a far more welcoming attitude towards the modern world, translating the lessons of William Morris and his followers into the very different age and spirit of Cubism and the Russian Ballet.

Consummate professionals, they were utterly dedicated to their art which, most unusually, stretched across many different media. Moreover they were artists of the purest type and singularly devoid of worldly ambitions. The artist and critic Lawrence Gowing recalled that, 'As far as I and my friends were concerned, their record was one of extraordinary generosity and of a peculiarly selfless enlightenment'.[2] As Quentin Bell observed of his mother,

> *Apart from maternal solicitudes, and being a grandmother, painting was the most important thing for her. If she had guests in the house, the guests could bloody well suffer before the painting. Even people she liked very much she would escape. The result was that she was very choosy about who came to the house, because it took away valuable painting time. She didn't want to be making polite conversation, or even gossip.*[3]

Following one unwanted visit in September 1927 she wrote to Roger Fry, explaining that she had painted a large sign saying 'To Charleston, OUT' and stuck it up at the bottom of a nearby field, presumably near the road, in order to deter the unwary.[4] It was, after all, a private house, and its occupants jealously guarded their privacy. Even Leonard and Virginia Woolf were not necessarily welcome if they came unannounced.[5]

Yet in Charleston's golden age from the mid-1920s to the mid-1930s there was a fairly constant stream of regular visitors alongside fellow artists and old Bloomsbury friends, including Frances Partridge, Janie Bussy, T.S. Eliot, Jean Renoir and many others. Shortly after moving, Vanessa wrote to Roger Fry:

> *It will be an odd life, but it seems to me it ought to be a good one for painting (...) It has been refaced with some kind of quite harmless stucco or plaster and has a creeper over it. The other sides are wonderful. I suppose it's 17th or 18th century (but my word doesn't go for much). Anyhow it's most lovely, very solid and simple, with flat walls in that lovely mixture of brick and flint that they use about here, and perfectly flat windows in the walls and wonderful tiled roofs. The pond is most beautiful, with a willow at one side and a stone or flint wall edging it all round the garden part, and a little lawn sloping down to it, with formal bushes on it. Then there's a small orchard and the walled garden like the Asheham one (...) The Omega dinner service looks most lovely on the dresser.*[6]

Returning to Charleston in August 1921 after a lengthy absence from the house, she explained in a letter to Duncan Grant how astonished she was

> *to find how much energy we spent on this place, how many tables and chairs and doors we painted and how many colour schemes we invented. Considering what a struggle it was to exist here at all, I can't think how we had so much surplus energy.*[7]

Dark corridors still give onto a sequence of rooms remarkable for the variety of moods they establish. There are no conventional murals at Charleston, and most of the atmosphere depends on generally muted large-scale abstract wall-painting, as in Duncan Grant's studio, the walls of which are filled with large hovering brown panels thinly and broadly brushed on, to marvellous effect, inside broad, pale pink borders. They perfectly complement the central focus of the fireplace with its beefy caryatids cheerfully flanking a big upright stove, just as the pale grey stencilled walls of the garden sitting-room prove ideal companions to another colourfully decorated fireplace.

It is against such large-scale backdrops that the rooms slowly and beguilingly reveal their contents, all of which are given space to breathe in a manner quite unlike the claustrophobically over-crowded atmosphere of most Victorian interiors. There is constant dialogue throughout the house between the furnishings, including the artists' hand-painted vases, lamp-stands, screens, cupboards, and decorated fireplaces, doors, and window embrasures, as well as comfortable homely furniture largely upholstered with their own fabrics. Many of the curtains and rugs are also to their own designs, as are the many examples of embroidery throughout the house, replete with their own intimate associations of the friends and family members who had worked them.

Installed only in 1939, the telephone was recognised as a necessary evil, a life-line which at the same time always threatened unwelcome intrusions and interruptions of their much cherished privacy. It was positioned directly behind Vanessa's place at the head of the dining table, and she was an adept at informing unwanted callers that she was not at home. In the days before the entire national telephone network was finally fully automated one had to dial the operator in order to be connected to remoter countryside lines, and in order to reach Charleston one asked for 'Ripe 265'. It always took a few moments before the old black bakelite telephone clicked into action. It still stands by the west facing window and I can never look at it without thinking of its uniquely far-away-sounding yet at the same time intimate ringing tone, as if one were getting through to another world of long-ago, as in a way one was. The number survives to this day, fossilised from an earlier technological age within the line which provides recorded information for visitors.

As Lawrence Gowing observed:

In a place like Charleston you can really see the sinews that hold the past to the future. That house is not only a beautiful thing (. . .) it is beautiful in its expression of a profound truth that cannot be expressed in any other way. The substance of tradition is social, real human sociability (. . .) When Vanessa spoke in her grave deep voice, in whose timbre the immanence of love and laughter always lurked, one was in no doubt that it was the beauty of painting

*that she held dear, as we must hold and keep it now. It is a domestic beauty,
like a family feeling: that is why it is felt to such advantage in that house.
At Charleston we were always in Vanessa's presence — with attention we
can imagine the amorous spell, which alone held together such an improbable
community for so long.*[8]

Duncan and Vanessa

According to Leonard Woolf,

*Vanessa in her thirties had something of the physical splendour which Adonis
must have seen when the Goddess suddenly stood before him. (...) I myself never
found her formidable, partly because she had the most beautiful speaking voice
that I have ever heard, and partly because of her tranquillity and quietude.
(The tranquillity was to some extent superficial; it did not extend deep down in
her mind, for there in the depths there was also an extreme sensitivity, a nervous
tension which had some resemblance to the mental instability of Virginia).*[9]

Given Duncan Grant's great physical beauty when young, together they made a most striking impression.

Ironically both Vanessa and Duncan suffered from jealousy which was similar in kind and degree, but not reciprocal. Vanessa was frequently afraid she would one day lose Duncan to a male lover, but she did not see that throughout his life, from David Garnett onwards, Duncan repeatedly fell most deeply in love with narcissistic heterosexual men whom he charmed but who were not attracted to him sexually or able to reciprocate his sexual love. They caused him pain, but ultimately presented no real threat to Vanessa's authority. Indeed, it is worth pointing out that while Duncan Grant and David Garnett are routinely referred to as 'lovers' throughout the literature of Bloomsbury, it is extremely doubtful if much in the way of sex ever took place between them.

Garnett was a vain and by every account energetically heterosexual man who was evidently wholly impervious to the different kinds of extreme anguish he managed to stir up in both Duncan and Vanessa. Duncan's besotted devotion hardly made them 'lovers', whilst Garnett's own account of his time at Charleston is highly evasive. His note to

Lytton Strachey at Christmas 1918 announcing his calculating intention to eventually marry Vanessa and Duncan's newly born daughter Angelica seems only too self-revealing.[10] He would possess both Duncan and Vanessa by default.

At the same time the rewards were great. Both could protect and support one another as artists within a predominantly literary-intellectual milieu which they both found more intimidating than they generally let on. They belonged to a pre-war avant-garde which was already a distant memory by the late 1920s. In such circumstances the risk of excessive social withdrawal was real for both of them, but rather more so for Vanessa who was by temperament the more reserved and retiring. Of all the central characters of Bloomsbury, Duncan Grant remains the most elusive. Lacking the publication of his letters, we do not see his view of Vanessa Bell or Virginia Woolf or any of the other members of the Bloomsbury group as clearly as we see their views of him. This has led to much misunderstanding, and he is sometimes depicted as a rather shallow, selfish person which is impossible to square with the loving devotion of everyone who ever knew him, with the sole exception of D.H. Lawrence, hardly a reliable witness. It is also reflected in the frequent tendency to look at his relationship with Vanessa only from her point of view, not from his.

Many later commentators appear to regret the failure of Vanessa's affair with Roger Fry, unable or unwilling to see that she could never have long shared or tolerated his primarily intellectual outlook and company, in spite of his great kindness. Fry may have had an important liberating effect on her sexually, but not artistically, and much as they both loved and admired him, she and Duncan preferred to hide their latest pictures when he visited their studios to circumvent discussions of their work from someone whose artistic judgement they did not respect as much as one another's. This must have been one important reason why the affair foundered. Besides, Vanessa did not take kindly to advice, even from artists such as Sickert whom she genuinely admired.[11]

The emotional need which informed her dependence on Duncan was not a late aberration, as many have seen it, but was forged from childhood and of the essence of her inner self, and it is difficult to imagine Vanessa capable of an adult relationship of which she was not fully in control. The many years of unprotected exposure to her father's constant displays of self-dramatising self-pity and emotional blackmail, coupled with his miserly bullying of her in matters of household management, together ensured her determination in later life to keep her own deepest feelings to herself, and made it difficult for her to accept male authority of any kind in any area of her life.

As Virginia commented of their long years cooped up with their father in Hyde Park Gate after their mother's death: 'The cruelty was that while we could see the future we were completely in the power of the past'.[12] Yet unlike her younger sister, Vanessa had received little in the way of parental encouragement in relation to her early ambitions, and she subsequently had to carve out her life and her career for herself on her own terms without any assistance from anyone. She had also shouldered much of the burden of her sister's early breakdowns. All these factors conspired to make her fiercely cherish her independence, yet unable to draw upon ordinary avenues of help and support. Duncan's unstinting care and loyalty may have been partly in recognition of this, just as Leonard Woolf responded protectively to Virginia's emotional constrictions. We should not blame him if he refused the option of a lifetime of chastity, or of a dishonest pretence of heterosexuality.

Like her mother, Vanessa had little capacity for self-reflection, and moreover was evidently vulnerable to what her daughter has described as 'the traditional bugbear of the Stephens, masochistic self-pity, handed down, it seemed, from one generation to the next'.[13] In a way she was too strong for her own good, and the mastery she displayed in hiding her feelings could make her seem cold and remote to those who did not know her well. When in later life Duncan was occasionally persuaded to show visitors around the house it was infinitely touching to hear him pointing out how 'this picture was painted by Mrs Bell' or 'that fireplace is by Mrs Bell', without ever drawing attention to any of his own work. One knew instinctively that had she survived him, this was just how she would have spoken of their joint achievements.

The house

Always somehow unexpected at the end of the turning from the long lane which winds its way between working fields from the A27 to Tilton and the old carriage-way along the foot of the Downs, Charleston suddenly seems to spring out of nowhere at the very last moment. Never static, its interiors, like its gardens, constantly changed and evolved over time, as rooms and furniture were decorated and redecorated, and pictures were changed and moved around. As John Russell notes, an 'inspired, life-giving untidiness was the mark of much of the house',[14] and in recent years the Charleston Trust has aimed as far as possible to preserve its relaxed and casual lived-in atmosphere. Fitted out with furniture which was variously purpose-made, inherited, or bought on European holidays, together with curious bits and pieces picked up for a song at local junk shops and transformed with startling inventiveness into conformity with the prevailing house style, it provides an enduringly eloquent reproach to the heavy ugliness of the 19th century and to the shoddiness of so much of the 20th.

Like every old house it is also a place of ghosts, and one reason why visitors so frequently return is surely the uncanny sense of proximity it affords to its former Bloomsbury inhabitants. Photographs demonstrate the extent to which the house was in fact largely dismantled during the initial restoration, and although the lumpy beds have remained un-slept in for over a quarter of a century, nonetheless the sense that their occupants might at any moment return is tangibly, and often unnervingly, felt. Above all, it is in Mollie Panter-Downes' felicitous phrase, an 'amorous' house.[15] An ensemble, and at the same time a sequence of rooms, each with its own distinct atmosphere, it is saturated with memories of family gatherings, birthday parties with fireworks, amateur dramatics, dressing-up, and so on.

The house and its place in the landscape have changed remarkably little in the course of the past century, and, in spite of the regrettable demolition of the adjacent granary in the early 1970s and new car-parking facilities, Charleston remains unnervingly like its former self. A house of artists and children, it retains much of its relaxed, unconventional spirit, though its characteristic smell of dogs, of oil paint, turps and rabbit size, of coffee and cheroots, has long since faded into the ether, leaving only the farmyard in one's nose. Duncan and Vanessa's approach was the antithesis of modern farm-conversions which aim to gut and transform defenceless old farmhouses into homogenised high-tech palaces of conspicuous consumption with no trace of much despised colour, let alone dusty old books or any sign of distinctively individual creative inner personal life. Its miraculously preserved air of benign homeliness only serves to enhance the fact that the style of decoration on display represents the finest surviving example of one of the very few important and original British contributions to European modern art. Its style is as distinct as that of Kent or Adam, and every bit as civilised and sophisticated.

It is a house of big gestures, reflecting, as Quentin Bell observed,

a desire to live comfortably without the complications that arise when decoration is used for status seeking, for nothing counts here but those intense pleasures of the eye the decorative arts can achieve.[16]

Its decor carries distant echoes of the Russian Ballet, but still more of the dry matte surface qualities of the Romanesque and early Renaissance painted interiors of the French and Italian churches which both Duncan and Vanessa so much admired, albeit translated into wholly modern terms. This was achieved by using gelatin to fix pure pigment to a chalk ground in just the right proportions, a difficult technique used to great effect throughout.[17] Charleston is as different as can be imagined from the richly austere interiors of Charles Rennie Mackintosh, yet it is none the less an equally valid and significant complementary expression of the excitement of early Modernism. It is a style deceptively easy to pastiche, yet of a quality impossible to duplicate.

The entrance hall

Early photographs show a small gabled entrance-porch, but this was removed during World War II when a new front door from a bombed house in London was installed, repainted in Vanessa's signature salmon-pink and grey. A glazed inner door opens into a compact tiled entrance hall with doors leading off on either side into the downstairs library and the dining-room, with a back door into the kitchen area ahead, and the big double doors of the main china cupboard on the left. Throughout the house the door-surrounds are painted matte dove-grey, a perfect foil to the rest of the decor. At the far left stands a plaster head by Gimond, which beautifully complements a wooden Chinese statue of an Earth God sitting on a small fret-worked chinoiserie table to the right, below a prettily framed Italian mirror. On a small table opposite stands the hand-bell sounded to announce meals. There are also several pictures, including an early 1920s watercolour copy by Duncan Grant of Cézanne's 1865 portrait of his wife from the collection of the Barnes Foundation in Philadelphia. Plain corridors on both floors hung with a wide variety of drawings and prints give onto the main rooms, the upper floor reached by carpeted stairs on the far right.

The kitchen

It is significant that the sensible working kitchen was from the outset felt to require decoration, rather than being left plain. It belongs with the rest of house, and this in itself tells us something important about the affectionate and mutually respectful worlds of all those who lived and worked here. It also reflects the transformation of social relations in the course of the 20th century, as increasing numbers of householders prepared their own food. It is, however, still clearly a traditional farmhouse kitchen, and most unlike the streamlined kitchens of the late 20th century which are so often largely theatres of social status and conspicuous consumption.

A large work table stands in the centre of the room beneath the first of several hanging semi-circular ceramic lamp-shades in the house which were made and decorated by Quentin Bell. Perforated all over its surface it throws light downwards as well as radiating tiny beams out and upwards in all directions, to delightful effect. The kitchen was a busy social space where the postman visited twice a day, and deliveries arrived from Lewes shop-keepers and the village shop in Firle. Fruit and vegetables also came from the garden. In the early years, ducks and hens had their own houses among the outbuildings, and rabbits were also bred for eating. Grace Higgens was housekeeper and worked here for 50 years, maintaining an unchanging routine. A large walk-in shelved pantry speaks of a world long before the availability of domestic refrigerators. Behind a door on the left, a staircase leads up to the Higgens' living area, known as High Holborn, on the west side of the attics. Grace retired in 1970, and is remembered here by the painted wall-tiles by Quentin Bell behind the Aga.

Clive Bell's study

Facing the pond, the downstairs study became a library after the arrival of Clive Bell's books in 1939. It contains the earliest surviving decorations in the house around the window by Vanessa Bell from 1916. They are strikingly different from the fireplace she so confidently decorated in the late 1920s, in her most strikingly original style, which is all the more important for its rarity, given the loss of so many of her other contemporary interiors. In the window-bay stands a fine tile-topped table by Duncan Grant from around 1930, decorated with a central vase of flowers, and nicely complemented by the fabric on the chairs, designed by Roger Fry and Duncan Grant. Above the central early 19th-century marquetry table is another of Quentin's hanging ceramic lampshades.

Originally the walls were left white, but were painted acid green by Nerissa Garnett in the early 1970s, supposedly in consultation with her grandfather Duncan Grant, though this is rather difficult to believe. The painted door by Duncan Grant is of two periods, the upper panel from around 1917 includes a jug full of hand-painted paper-flowers from the Omega Workshop on a shelf in front of a view of the barns outside, as if the intervening walls were transparent. A lower panel was damaged when the room was used as a school-room, and was repainted by Grant with a tumbling dancer in the 1950s at a time when he was particularly delighted by performances by Chinese State acrobats. There are also lots of interesting pictures, including a 1908 drawing of Clive Bell by Henry Lamb and an etching by Derain given to him by the artist, as well as Frederick Etchells' brilliant post-Impressionist tribute to the art of

English hunting scenes from around 1912. Although Clive was a frequent visitor to Charleston, by 1939 he and Vanessa had not lived together for some 25 years, and his return must have taken some getting used to.

The dining room

Although it now seems such a unified set-piece, the decoration of the dining room evolved only slowly into its present form. The wide recessed hearth was opened up in the mid-1920s, and the old Staffordshire figure in the central niche could hardly have a happier home. The large central circular table was introduced in 1934. Its now poignantly worn surface was painted by Vanessa Bell in 1952, replacing an earlier design. It is surrounded by a complete set of cane-backed Chinese-red Omega Workshop chairs which give the lie to the idea that nothing from the Omega was ever enduringly well made. The stencilled walls were Duncan Grant's idea in 1939 and executed by him together with Vanessa, Angelica Garnett and Quentin Bell, forming a perfect background for the many fine pictures, especially effective at night in the disseminated light from Quentin's ceramic lampshade. The paintings include two early works by Vanessa, and Duncan's copy (done in the Uffizi Gallery in 1905) of Piero della Francesca's famous profile-portrait of Federigo da Montefeltro, as well as his important 1913 portrait of Lytton Strachey at Asheham. This is flanked by two small pictures, an exquisitely beautiful contemporary still-life of primulas in a vase inscribed to Duncan Grant by Vanessa Bell in the late 1930s, and his own terrific contemporary oil sketch of the household cat.

A glass cabinet from Hyde Park Gate houses old decanters and brandy glasses, and it was here that Clive regularly left white chocolate for nightly dispersal to the children. Breakfast was informal, after which Vanessa would retire to the kitchen for domestic business, before rejoining Duncan to work in their studios.[18] People only changed for dinner if there were guests. Food was brought in from the adjacent kitchen through the side door hidden behind Duncan's richly brocaded Clouds fabric a charmingly theatrical effect. The curtains were chosen by Vanessa, who had a great love of chintz. A particularly nice effect is struck by the juxtaposition of an ornate Venetian side-table with its elegantly cabriole legs and the small, plain mid-18th century piano opposite, which Duncan inherited from his father. Though not much used in later years I recall Duncan's great pleasure listening to a French friend of mine playing Chopin on it, and his amusement as Philippe struggled to confine his hands to the tiny keyboard.

The upstairs library

The main staircase leads up to the first floor, with a suite of rooms to the left which were converted for use by Clive Bell from 1939 until his death in 1964. Initially used by Vanessa as her bedroom between 1918 and 1939, the library walls were originally a deep Prussian blue. She supervised the change to black and Venetian red around 1918, suggesting much about her affection for the subdued low-key colour schemes of the early aesthetic movement, and one thinks in particular of the work, now mainly destroyed, of E.W. Godwin. Between 1916 and 1917, Grant painted her lurcher below the north-facing window, with a beady-eyed cockerel above it. A little later he added the Piero della Francesca-inspired figures on the back of the door. The predominantly grey chintz curtains at the north-facing window were of Vanessa's choosing. The main piece of furniture is Grant's 1927 bookcase, a refugee in 1939 from Clive Bell's London flat at 50 Gordon Square. With its two splendidly buxom seated female lutanists, it is the sole survivor of the furnishings of a whole network of London flats and homes which were decorated by Duncan and Vanessa between 1910 and the late 1930s. The room also contains two of a set of six Venetian chairs upholstered in Duncan's 1932 'Grapes' fabric, and although they are not readily visible, many of the books on the crowded shelves wear startlingly modern Bloomsbury-made abstract collaged covers.

Clive Bell's bedroom

A huge magnolia grandiflora outside admits a subterranean, greenish light at the far end of the room first used as a nursery, then as Angelica's bedroom. The foot- and head-board of the Louis XVI bed were decorated by Vanessa in about 1950. The bed was much more comfortable to sleep in than those in the spare bedroom. The blue fitted carpet is now a copy of the original which was imported from Bell's London flat, provides a metropolitan air quite unlike that given by the informal rugs and kelims elsewhere in the house. The corner cupboard was painted by Duncan in 1925, and there are many pictures that had been given to Clive by French artist-friends, including drawings by Derain and de Segonzac. The best picture is Frederick Etchells' superb 1912 *Entry Into Jerusalem* bought by Duncan. In such surroundings it is easy to miss the full significance of the large floor-to-ceiling collage to the left of the bed, which was undertaken by Vanessa in around 1917 to disguise the site of a former door. It may justly be considered as her largest abstract painting, and is a major work of its time. Hers also are the yellow beams.

Maynard Keynes' room

Regularly used by Maynard Keynes from 1919 until his marriage in 1925, the adjacent bedroom was occupied by Quentin Bell in the late 1930s and he left his mark in the stained glass panel in the door and another of his central ceramic lampshades. The room now contains an important 1913-14 Omega Workshops lily-pond table by Duncan Grant which replaces a similar example formerly recorded here. It stands in front of a beautiful mid-19th-century cane-backed Sussex settle of the type which so inspired William Morris. To the left of the window is a plain low linen-chest exuberantly decorated by Duncan Grant in 1917, with a humorous tribute to Ovid in the form of Leda and the Duck on the exposed underside of the lid, and a vivacious Whitman-esque post-Impressionist male swimmer on the front. However perhaps the most remarkable object is Vanessa's bed (now placed in this room), decorated by Duncan in 1917, with its head presided over by Morpheus the god of sleep, and her initials in a circular cartouche on the reverse. With its hypnotic blue eyes, its nailed-on wooden nose and brow, and its delirious false-marbling, it is one of the most strikingly imaginative pieces of furniture of its day. The walls are entirely undecorated, save for the pale grey wainscoting.

Duncan Grant's bedroom

At the far end of the upstairs corridor on the left is Duncan Grant's bedroom, which was at first used by Vanessa as a studio. The walls were originally green but have long been repainted a chalky white containing traces of black and burnt sienna, with dark red wainscoting.[19] By 1917 it was in use as his bedroom and in that year Vanessa decorated the fireplace and its two superb flanking doors, just as he had decorated her bedroom. At the time she wrote to Roger Fry that she was not 'doing anything very startling – only pots of flowers and marbled circles'.[20] They are in fact amongst the loveliest things in the house, and make up one the greatest tours-de-force of early Modernist decor in Britain. In the mid-1920s she added the decorations to the window embrasure, as well as the tiled hearth and fire-screen. The drawing above the writing-desk is by Delacroix and was a gift from Maynard Keynes from the sale of Degas' studio contents in 1918, which Grant had encouraged him to attend to buy pictures for the National Gallery.

The low embroidered music-stool with its elaborate musical instruments was designed by Duncan in 1924, and was worked by his mother Ethel, as was the settle at the window. The latter was designed rather more simply by Vanessa in 1943, since Mrs Grant was by then losing her sight, and it has much in keeping with her book-covers for the Hogarth Press. Ethel also worked the central rug with its goldfish, a motif Duncan frequently used in his decorations, including the small 1917 mosaic immediately outside the downstairs studio. A noble lead bust of Vanessa by Marcel Gimond from 1920-21 presides over the room from the top of a 19th-century French chest of drawers flanked by two delightfully unlikely Irish upright gilt and scarlet prie-dieu chairs, richly crusted with beadwork, which caught Duncan's eye sometime around 1918. The cylindrical wooden bedside lamp-stand was decorated by Duncan in the late 1930s, and makes a pair with the one in the downstairs sitting-room. There are several fine pictures, including Vanessa's beautiful 1913 *Still-life with Beer Bottle*. Behind the left-hand door is a small dressing-room with a row of big, jolly 18th-century-style black silhouette portraits of Grant family members. A small side-table carries a lively scene of

Orion riding a very goldfish-like dolphin, which was painted in around 1945 on top of a much earlier scheme still visible on the sides and legs. 'Dolphin' was Virginia's well-known nickname for Vanessa.

The spare bedroom

With its two severely plain Heal's single beds, the spare bedroom opposite Duncan Grant's bedroom houses a motley assortment of old furniture, much of which was decorated at various times over the years, as well as a large dressing-table from Hyde Park Gate which is the only piece in the house which doesn't quite fit in with its surroundings. The walls were painted by Vanessa in 1936 in her favourite salmon-pink and dove-grey, together with the delightful window embrasure with its flanking lilies in vases. The cupboard door on the left of the room was painted by Angelica Garnett at the same time. There were printed cotton Indian throws on the beds decades before such things became widely available and popular. For many years Duncan Grant's copy of Gainsborough's *Baillie Family Group* dominated the room. There is still a fine portrait of Julian Bell as a child, painted at Asheham in 1912 by the French artist Henri Doucet, who was killed in action in 1915, as well as an exceptionally good 1918 still-life by Edward Wolfe, a 1923 impression of Sickert's *Jack Ashore* (a gift to Duncan from the artist), and Vanessa's magnificent 1947 *Still-life with Plaster Head*.

Vanessa Bell's attic studio

Reached by a second narrow staircase which passes a box-room under the eaves, a series of attics originally provided the housekeeper's living-space, and nurseries. The most northerly of these was converted into a studio for Vanessa in 1939 with the addition of a wide five-light window. With a commanding view over the walled garden, and stretching without interruption across the Sussex Weald to the distant rising sandstone hills of the Ashdown forest, it provided her with a perfect refuge from the busy life of the rest of the house. At the same time she vacated her former first-floor bedroom for use by Clive as his library, and moved downstairs to a newly constructed bedroom on the ground floor.

The sitting room

Returning to the ground floor, a narrow L-shaped downstairs corridor leads from the entrance hall to Duncan Grant's studio at the far end, and gives onto the garden-facing sitting-room and Vanessa's bedroom. Hung with many small pictures, it was always plain white with dove-grey wainscoting and doors. The first room one comes to is the sitting room, with French windows opening directly onto the gravelled garden terrace and a small side window facing the pond. It is the most elaborate of all the interiors at Charleston, and was doubtless always the 'best' room in the house, with its eloquently stencilled dove-grey walls of 1945, to which Duncan Grant's yellow linen pelmet and curtains, designed for the Music Room exhibition of 1932, provide a perfect foil. They are admirably complemented by the floor-to-ceiling chintz curtains at the French windows, the fabric for which was bought by Vanessa at the Chintz Shop on Praed Street in London.[21]

The room's main focus however is Duncan Grant's 1928 over-mantel, with a central oval still-life replacing a former sea-view, flanked and supported by two life-size seated classical maidens, who are very much sisters to the slightly later screen by Vanessa, formerly at Monks House. Just below them on the mantelpiece is a small grinning French 19th-century ceramic lion, flanked by two shapely blue and white Italian vases which echo the voluptuous forms of the figures painted behind them. Meanwhile to the right of the fireplace is a small wooden log-box painted by Duncan Grant in around 1917 with alternating dancing figures and angel-musicians, revisiting the type of imagery often used by Burne-Jones and other late Victorian designers in full-blooded early 20th-century style.

In the alcove to the left of the fireplace hangs an important late self-portrait by Vanessa Bell, which was bought from the sale of Lord Clark's collection in 1984. Copies of the originals by Picasso and Vlaminck bought in Paris before World War I and which had to be sold after World War I speak mutely and poignantly of straitened circumstances. Two large cross-stitch cushions designed by Vanessa add a note of comfort to the big old armchairs, which are unusual at Charleston in not being covered in Bloomsbury-designed fabrics. Above the radiator by the door is a tiled shelf by Vanessa, from which hangs a wool and bead curtain made by her in 1928 to hide the radiator behind. On a small card-table at the far end of the room stands a small plaster by Renoir of his son Claude at the age of seven, like a shrine to childhood.

Vanessa Bell's bedroom

With new French windows giving onto the garden and large double-doors into Duncan Grant's studio beyond, Vanessa's bedroom was converted in 1939 from a former substantial dairy-cum-larder, and she died here on 7 April 1961 in her austerely plain Heal's bed. Her children look down at her from portraits on the walls, and the dominant feature in the room is the tall cupboard which she must have painted shortly after arriving at Charleston.

Its doors are decorated with 16 vertically aligned yellow spheres, eight on each door, with pink and dark-red detailing against a grey background. It is one of her most satisfying works, and perfectly embodies the spirit of Charleston. It was to be immensely prophetic of her later decorative work, which so often returns to recapitulate and elaborate this most basic and elemental of motifs, so appropriate to her own personality. It formerly housed her much-treasured collection of bits of old fabric and stuffs gathered from her travels, including a blue silk jacket designed in 1917 for Jacques Copeau's Paris production of Maurice Maeterlinck's play *Pelléas et Mélisande,* which briefly transferred to New York in the following year.

Two exquisite 1908 studies of Julian as a baby hang by her desk, and by the door is a 1910 self-portrait by Duncan, very different in style from his jolly *Spanish Lady* of around 1930 hanging over the bath, which is concealed behind a fantastic 1913 Omega Workshops screen, also by Duncan – as daringly advanced as anything of its date in England. He repaired some damage to the purely abstract geometric side in the 1960s. There is also another embroidery-framed mirror designed by Duncan in much the same style as the slightly earlier mirror, now in the dining-room at Monks House, which Virginia adored. There were formerly two such mirrors at Monks House and three at Charleston, providing one of many such levels of dialogue between the two houses.

Duncan Grant's studio

In the summer of 1925 a new purpose-built studio designed by Roger Fry was added on the site of a former yard and chicken-run facing onto the garden. For many years shared by Duncan and Vanessa, it is a large airy room with a high gabled roof and raised north-facing windows letting in a maximum of light, yet preventing the interior from being overlooked from outside. Although designed for work it proved equally amenable to relaxed social life, focused around an upright stove in front of a recess lined with tiles painted by Vanessa with abstracted flowers against a sponged blue background. After her death in 1961 Duncan spent most of his time in this studio and it slowly accumulated its present appearance. It is an appropriately inward-looking room, in which nothing is too overpowering.

Angelica Garnett has pointed out that the walls are 'the antithesis of the dazzling white usually considered necessary for a studio'.[22] The borders of softly pale pink, grey and green were painted first, while the large, loosely washed brown central panels were seemingly added in the 1940s. As usual at Charleston the main accent is provided by the fireplace, which is of two periods. The upper decorative panels were painted soon after the studio was built, but the present colourfully nubile male caryatids painted on panels below are 1930s replacements for similar earlier figures painted directly onto the underlying plaster.

To the right of the fireplace stands a large glazed 18th-century Dutch walnut cabinet, inherited from W.M. Thackeray, which displays many examples of their painted china, balanced on the other side of the room by a tall, framed embroidered panel designed by Duncan Grant and worked by his mother between 1924 and 1926. It characteristically translates something of the late-Roman mosaic arch-decorations found at Ravenna into the house-style of modern Bloomsbury decorative art. A severely plain bentwood armchair from Heal's was a rather mischievous gift to Vanessa from Virginia in 1937, and is sister to two similar chairs still at Monks House. Roundly condemned by Sickert when he saw it in her London studio, it seems perfectly at home in these surroundings and reminds one of the many different currents at work in English art and design in that decade.

As in all the rooms there are many pictures by and of family and friends, while Stephen Tomlin's 1931 plaster bust of Virginia Woolf stares out imperiously from the top of a substantial early 19th-century chest of drawers, where she keeps good company with whisky bottles and glasses and studio bric-a-brac. It is the only image of her in the house. A lead cast of the bust stands on a low retaining wall in the garden at Monks House, together with a later bust of Leonard at the other end of the same wall. She is perfectly matched by the plaster cast of a sixth-century Chinese Goddess of Mercy above the fireplace, the original of which belonged to Roger Fry.

The end wall is flanked by two narrow upright Italian fairground figures bought by Duncan in Ravenna in 1913 from the memorably named Dante Paradiso, 'a young man of exquisite beauty and a charming smile' according to Vanessa Bell.[23] Between them is a large oval mirror which once belonged to Sickert, as did the chaise-longue beneath. Along the window shelf stand several vases, two of which were painted by Duncan in Tunisia while on holiday with Maynard Keynes in 1914. The shapely grey and mushroom-coloured gramophone cabinet was decorated by Vanessa for the Music Room exhibition in 1932, from which there is also a small cupboard at Monks House (*see p.43*). A striking male nude painted by Duncan in Rome in the 1930s now stands on the main studio easel, but it was not displayed there in his lifetime. A small top-lit open recess to the right gives onto doors opening directly onto the garden.

At the far end of the room a glazed door opens out under a rickety vine-covered pergola into a small walled yard. Long known as Grant's Folly, it contains a small square central pond, and is planted with periwinkle, bluebells and small black irises. The old chicken house in the far right-hand corner was converted into a pottery in 1939. The figs around the walls have been rather drastically cut back in recent years. A trellis immediately outside the studio door into the back garden carries another old vine. In good years Grace used to make jam from the grapes.

The garden

Though lacking its former splendidly gnarled and twisted apple trees, the garden is still very much as it was, hidden safely inside its buttressed traditional brick and flint retaining walls. The basic plan, with a front lawn and gravel paths, was laid out by Roger Fry, but modified by Duncan and Vanessa who introduced smaller flower-beds and more paths. It was an essential resource for still-lives, and ensured idyllic views from the house painted at every season in the endless dialogue of inside and outside, both physical and psychological, that is such a characteristic of Bloomsbury art, and one of its most abidingly inspiring pleasures.

Fry had worked with Gertrude Jekyll on the design and planting of his gardens at Durbins, and the garden at Charleston, though less formal, is also in the broad tradition of Arts-and-Crafts gardens in which

> *paths and pergolas carried the architectural lines of the house into the garden setting, and semi-glazed doors, generous verandas and terraces diminished the boundaries between the living space of the house and the garden beyond.*[24]

Dense planting is barely contained within the architectural layout, and includes several of Jekyll's signature plants such as lamb's ears and *hydrangea petiolaris* which Duncan especially liked. Vanessa had visited Sissinghurst, but there is no trace of Vita Sackville-West's influence at Charleston.

Duncan and Vanessa spent a lot of time and energy on the garden and it frequently appears in their letters. In April 1924 Duncan wrote to Vanessa from Charleston to inform her that their gardener, Mr Stevens,

> *is going to give us some stocks and marigolds later but says it is too late to plant roses this year, so we shall have to put other things in the terrace beds. I am very much tempted to spend a pound or two on lily bulbs. I have a catalogue of autumn flowering lilies which sound too lovely for words. What do you think? In any case I am going to buy a collection of late flowering gladiolus which (...)*

are quite cheap and very easy to grow – one can have clumps of them. Also I am going to sow some sun flowers.[25]

In 1933 Vanessa supervised a red planting with dahlias, hollyhocks, scabious, salpiglossis and zinnias, and her upstairs studio was stocked with well-thumbed old seed and plant catalogues. Today it remains essentially an English cottage garden, with lilies, red hot pokers, hellebores, aquilegia, asters, campanula, cranesbill, bleeding hearts, honeysuckle, lupins, poppies, phlox, and of course masses of roses. There is also a large orchard beyond, and one should recall that Sussex had for centuries been famous for its figs.

In the far western corner a rather more formal note is struck by a bricked area nicknamed the Piazza, with delightful mosaics made by Quentin Bell in 1946 from broken crockery, tiles and so on, to which he added a small semicircular pool with a fountain and mask in 1958. With its pond providing limitless potential for naval adventures, the garden was also of course a paradise for children, as eloquently described by both Angelica and Quentin.[26]

Getting there National grid ref. TQ493065
- Charleston is open from Easter to the end of October from Wednesday to Sunday. Opening hours vary and visitors should check by telephone or consult the website. There is a shop and tearoom.
- **Website:** www.charleston.org.uk
- **Visitor information:** 01323 811625.
- **Office:** 01323 811626.
- **By road:** Charleston is signposted on the right of the A27 Brighton to Eastbourne road between the villages of Firle and Selmeston.
- **Cycling:** View the National Cycle Network website: www.sustrans.org.uk
- **By rail:** Berwick is the nearest station. The walk to Charleston takes about an hour. Lewes station is some 4 miles (6 kilometres) away and taxis are available outside.
- **By bus:** The 125 service runs between Lewes bus station and Firle. Call Traveline for the times of services: 0870 608 2608 or visit their website: www.travelinesoutheast.org.uk

BERWICK CHURCH

AN EVOCATION OF WARTIME SUSSEX

The village of Berwick lies some three kilometres east of Charleston along the ancient bridleway which skirts the northerly escarpment of the Downs a few hundred metres south of the house. Set on a small hill with commanding views and well screened by trees, Berwick church stands in an attractive churchyard with an unusual number of excellent late 20th-century carved gravestones, which is also home to a Bronze Age barrow on the north side. Apart from its sweeping roofs and its plain early 17th-century west tower with a typical shapely Sussex broach-spire it is not a particularly attractive building, especially inside. The former medieval north aisle was demolished in 1743, reflecting the little church's then decrepit state, and it was heavily over-restored in the 1850s under the direction of the architect Henry Woodyer, who entirely rebuilt the chancel and added the eccentric north arcade and most of the rather clunky detail throughout. The Victorian nave windows were blown out by a bomb in 1944 and replaced by clear glass, providing an unusual and welcome effect of transparency on both sides.

Besides a much-restored gabled 14th-century tomb-recess on the north side of the chancel, the best monument in the church is now sadly hidden away under the tower and entirely blocked from sight. Of black and white marble and from a London workshop, it commemorates a 17th-century rector, the Reverend John Nutt (died 1656) and his wife, who are represented by two rather flat-faced busts in oval niches gazing for the foreseeable future at the south side of a large organ-case only millimetres from their noses. The only other feature of note is the ancient Norman tub font, older by far than the church in which it now stands. In such circumstances one can only be thankful for the murals and other mid-20th-century furnishings which provide a spiritual focus it certainly previously lacked.

Duncan Grant had apparently long cherished the possibility of decorating Berwick church, and we owe the realisation of his wishes to the enlightened patronage of Bishop George Bell of Chichester (no relation to the Bells), who was enthroned in 1929. A pioneering champion of modern ecclesiastical art, his attention was drawn to the artists of Charleston by Sir Charles Reilly, a friend of Duncan Grant's Aunt Violet and a former professor of architecture at Liverpool University, who had retired to Brighton.[1] The possibility was first suggested to Duncan in late 1940 and by January 1941 he and Vanessa were ready with initial plans for murals.

Almost inevitably a tragicomedy of obstacles ensued, but these were happily resolved largely due to the intervention of Frederick Etchells, an old colleague of theirs from the days of the Omega Workshops who had gone on to become a well-known designer of Anglican church fittings and furnishings. Although initially doubtful, he was quickly persuaded of the scheme's virtues, and after an official church hearing, objections to a faculty (authorisation) were overruled in October 1941, allowing work to proceed. The murals were eventually installed in 1943 and a service of dedication was held that October. Bands of colour were added to the edge of the Victorian chancel arch a few months later.[2]

Such an ambitious plan was a most remarkable thing to attempt at the height of the war, with air combats taking place daily overhead, and the entire project represented an impressive assertion of confidence in the enduring values of parish and indeed of national life at a time of such considerable adversity. Funds were forthcoming from Lord Clark, Maynard Keynes and others, including the department-store owner Peter Jones. Supporting the project, which was in any case hardly expensive, seemed in its way like part of the war effort, and the decorations at Berwick remain a uniquely poetic expression of Britain in wartime, the more moving for the way in which they embody a profound awareness of the historical traditions and continuities of Christian art, at the very moment when European civilisation was facing the greatest threat in its history.

This was the grim backdrop against which the scheme was conceived and executed. It was all the more notable for the fact that none of the artists involved were practising Christians, and that they came from a cultural background which was particularly hostile to all forms of jingoism and narrowly patriotic nationalism. Indeed, it is precisely the way in which the Berwick church decorations assert a national identity felt to be imperilled, without resorting to xenophobia, which makes the resulting interior all the more moving and effective.

The initial plans concerned the decoration of both sides of the chancel arch, and the two nave arcades. Later additions included a pulpit and a screen and a large image of Christ on the cross at the west end, together with other work in the chancel, including contributions by both Quentin Bell and Angelica Garnett. Bishop Bell was aware of the ancient traditions of mural painting in Sussex churches, of which a few splendid, if faded, examples can be seen at Clayton, Coombes, Hardham and elsewhere. These, ironically, owe their partial survival to their having been whitewashed over during the Reformation. The strong assertion of confidence in wall painting which the project embodied was in its way a defiant challenge to the imminent threat of a new and still more devastating form of iconoclasm associated with the menace of Nazism.

War art

In 1940 Duncan Grant worked briefly in Plymouth as an official war artist appointed by the War Artists' Advisory Committee, but the requirements of documentary accuracy proved a barrier to his imaginative talents and his resulting painting of sailors at a gunnery lesson was virtuous but unremarkable. The decoration of Berwick church was to be a much more personal contribution, drawing on rather different skills and inspiration. Working in a neighbouring barn lent for the purpose by

Maynard Keynes (who leased Tilton, not far from Charleston), Duncan and Vanessa painted onto large plasterboard panels which were subsequently attached to the surface of the church walls. They chose as their subject matter images from the heart of Christian art – Christ in Glory above the chancel arch, as he had appeared in most medieval parish churches, together with the Annunciation and the Nativity in the nave.

Unveiled in the dark days of 1943, the Berwick church murals have been overlooked in subsequent accounts of British cultural responses to World War II, not having been properly identified for what they are – an impressive and indeed visionary example of engaged war art, though not commensurate with the type of worthy factual painting with which official war art is generally associated. It is much more instructive to see them on a par with the contemporary wartime films of Michael Powell and Emeric Pressburger, especially their intensely poetic, allegorical wartime propaganda film, *A Canterbury Tale*. Filmed in 1943 in and around the devastated city of Canterbury, it evokes a vision of village life which could, like the murals at Berwick, be accused of sentimentality, but only by those with an extraordinarily blinkered view of the past and the emotions of wartime.

The murals at Berwick move us today precisely because of their quiet and touching evocation of wartime Sussex; Bishop Bell, the Rector of Berwick, and three representatives of the armed services kneel facing one another on either side of the chancel arch against the serene yet threatened local landscape spread out behind them, beneath Grant's majestic vision of Christ. The servicemen were modelled by local villagers including a son of the local station-master who was killed in action at Caen in 1944. In the great majority of medieval images of Christ in Glory, he is seen presiding over the reception of the Saved into the heavenly New Jerusalem on one side, facing the Damned as they are herded into the jaws of Hell by hideous demons and devils. Grant's view was significantly different. Hell is implied but not depicted as the wider enemy threat, and heaven by the simple beauty of the South Downs.

In a similar way Vanessa's Nativity scene is populated by local people, including the Higgens's young son John, and a local farmhand as one of the shepherds. The Christmas story is presented inside a barn looking out onto the same Downs seen on the chancel arch and outside the church itself, exactly like a traditional Christmas play still happily performed and attended annually in most churches by local parishioners and their children. One is also quietly reminded of the masque-like pageant of English history which is the central focus of Virginia Woolf's final novel, published posthumously in 1942.

Such correspondences between their work was not, I think, in any way calculated, but simply resulted from the way in which the artists worked. As Angelica Garnett points out of her parents, 'each was magnetized by the other because of their capacity for creating something that was unforeseen and original, giving them the magic power to produce a world of their own'.[3] This is not then political art in a narrow sense, but art which nonetheless responded spontaneously and imaginatively to the time and circumstances of its making, just as in the 1950s Duncan's decorations in the Russell chantry in Lincoln cathedral may be seen in part as a response to the vicious media-led homophobic witch-hunts which took place throughout the decade.

Christ in Glory

In most medieval images of Christ in Glory he sits enthroned above a celestial orb symbolising the entire created universe, but at Berwick he is depicted against a golden disc, the ancient image of the life-giving sun which the church had adapted to its own uses, like so many other aspects of pre-Christian belief. It is all the more appropriate bearing in mind the Great Antiphon sung, as Jacquetta Hawkes points out, on 21 December, pleading:

> *O Day-spring, Brightness of the Light eternal, and Sun of Justice, come and enlighten those who sit in darkness and the shadow of death.*[4]

As early as 1911 Grant had shown considerable interest in the conventions of medieval painting, as is apparent in his experimental use of the early Gothic technique of 'damp-fold' to represent the volume of clothed bodies in his large mural panel *Football*, now in the collection of Tate

Britain. The figure of Christ at Berwick follows the same Byzantine-inspired tradition which had informed Giotto, as well as the 12th-century Sussex artists who worked at Clayton and Coombes. In their depictions of the subject he opens his arms wide to the whole world rather than raising a hand in judgement over the souls of the dead. Between this heavenly domain and our own are four large, splendid angels hovering in adoration at his throne. As solid as the angels of Piero della Francesca and similarly robed, their mid-air dance has much in common with that of the angels of Tintoretto and Veronese, representing an inspired Bloomsbury reconciliation of the traditions of Tuscan and Venetian art. The image of the kneeling local servicemen seen against the backdrop of the Downs was evidently admired by the stained-glass artist Hugh Easton, who borrowed the motif for his 1947 War Memorial window in the south aisle of St Mary the Virgin at Willingdon near Eastbourne.

The Annunciation and the Nativity

The Annunciation on the north side of the nave takes place against the backdrop of the walled garden at Charleston. The date of the Annunciation is 23 March, and the beds are appropriately wintry with the suggestion of the fertility of spring on the way. In medieval poetry and devotions the image of the *hortus conclusus* or walled garden was widely associated with the Virgin Mary, but one suspects that Vanessa's choice was intuitive rather than historical, like everything we see at Berwick – with the possible exception of Quentin Bell's altar-painting of the supper at Emmaus.

Lacking a precise Biblical description, the Annunciation has been represented in many different ways, often seemingly determined by formal considerations. Thus in vertical formats, Mary and the angel usually, though by no means always, stand, whilst in horizontal versions, as at Berwick, they tend to kneel or Mary is seated. Modelled by Angelica, her mother's depiction of the Virgin shows her sinking meekly to her knees, whilst the angel follows an ancient formula with one arm raised in salutation like a classical orator, though here unusually he raises his left rather than his right hand. In most Annunciation scenes Mary either crosses her hands across her chest in supplication, or raises the palm of one hand towards her unexpected angelic visitor. There is no obvious precedent for Mary's posture at Berwick, and her gesture of meek assent with one hand turned towards her chest seems above all Victorian and may perhaps reflect a memory of the not dissimilar gesture in Burne-Jones' version of the subject in the collection of the Lady Lever Art Gallery in Liverpool, in which the standing figure of the Virgin was modelled by Vanessa's own mother, Julia Jackson.

It is characteristic of Vanessa's approach that the incarnation is effected not by the intervention of the Holy Spirit in the form of a dove, or by similarly miraculous rays of divine light, but simply by the wintry light falling on her right side. The Nativity is similarly depicted within the familiar conventions of Italian art for which there are countless precedents, with the animals in the stable represented only by their heads peering amiably at the sacred proceedings.

The pulpit

Painted by Vanessa in 1944, the pulpit originally featured three standing archangels very much in the style of Piero della Francesca, but they were vandalised beyond repair in 1962. There has been some discussion of the authorship of the present pulpit decorations, but finished studies by Duncan Grant exist for the two panels with flowers in rounded vases. On close examination it is clear that the two flanking panels at either end are by Vanessa Bell, while the central panel with a tapering chalice-shaped vase is a later work by Duncan Grant, perhaps with Angelica Garnett. The decorative vocabulary is instantly recognisable, and Vanessa's exceptionally beautiful panel on the far right-hand side, incorporating her favourite salmon-pink and dove-grey, may be compared to her dust-jackets for the Hogarth Press, and also to the vases of flowers which flank the window of the spare bedroom at Charleston. The roses and stylised lilies on Duncan's panels stand in a direct line of descent from such earlier work as the 1920s three-panelled screen and the tall embroidered panel which are both in his studio, and the beautiful embroidered mirror-frames at both Charleston and Monks House. Meanwhile the rounded vases are direct transcriptions of a two-handled vase thrown by Phyllis Keyes in Lewes in around 1930, closely following an original brought back from Tunisia by Duncan in 1914. It still stands on the window-ledge in his studio and appears in many still-lives.

The Crucifixion
In April 1944 Duncan painted a large image of Christ on the cross to hang at the west end of the church, its chalice-shaped background emphasising the eucharistic significance of the Crucifixion. Significantly it is not the suffering Christ of the later middle ages, but the more ancient image of Christ alive and triumphant and reigning from the cross.[5]

The rood screen
Before the reformation every parish church had a rood screen between the nave, which was used for many parish purposes, and the chancel, which was the preserve of the clergy. The rood screen added in 1944 at Berwick is delightfully simple and entirely traditional, as was appropriate in such a location. At the dado level Duncan painted four roundels depicting the labours of the months, a motif frequently found throughout the middle ages in both religious and secular settings. They are translated here into charming vignettes, one of which represents summer, showing a boy up a ladder placing apples into a tall basket carried on a girl's head – another quiet reference to the art of Piero at San Francesco in Arezzo by which Duncan had been so impressed in 1905. On the front of the central door-panels he painted the pond at Charleston at dawn and sunset, referring to Genesis 8, v.22. On the other side of the screen, facing east, Quentin Bell employed his considerable skills in six panels illustrating the sacraments of Baptism, Confirmation, Confession, Holy Communion, Marriage and Last Rights, all set in a charmingly idealised mid-Victorian Sussex, close in spirit to Mrs Gaskell's Cranford.

The chancel
The chancel was mainly decorated by Quentin Bell in various stages. High up on the west face of the chancel arch is his large painting of the

parable of the Wise and Foolish Virgins, part of the original decorations installed in 1943 and something of a tribute to Burne-Jones's *Golden Stairs* of 1880, now in the collection of Tate Britain. On the north wall is a small grisaille wall-painting of two angels holding up a shield with the words *Domine Dirige Nos* ('Lord guide us'), while on the opposite wall is a chalice filled with lilies and crowned with a wreath. The 1944 altar frontal with its central image of the Virgin and Child was designed by Duncan and embroidered by his mother. The decoration of the pelmet and flanking pilasters recalls his work on the pulpit and elsewhere.

The Supper at Emmaus

In 1944 Quentin Bell painted a reredos to stand behind the altar at the east end of the church, intended to draw the attention of the congregation during the Communion service, when much of what is going on concerns the priest and is largely inaudible and invisible to everyone else. At first sight 'The Supper At Emmaus' might seem a rather strange choice of subject, perhaps reflecting Quentin's strong attraction to the supernatural. The story is one of the strangest in the New Testament. At the end of St Luke's Gospel we read of two of Christ's followers walking from Jerusalem to the nearby village of Emmaus discussing the crucifixion which had taken place three days earlier, and the discovery earlier that morning of the empty tomb. It is a story of mis-recognition, followed by revelation, and then loss.

In the rectangular version of the subject by a follower of Velasquez in the National Gallery of Ireland, the supper is seen in the distance through the hatchway of a kitchen in the foreground, where a tired-looking black girl is shown at work putting away plates and cooking utensils. It is this format of a picture-within-a-picture that Quentin Bell has loosely followed here, but with the significant difference that behind the table at which the meal is taking place a verandah opens up directly onto the South Downs, much as they appear behind the church, as if we were looking right through the painting and the east wall behind it.

The painting thus opens up a sense of a continuous space between our world and that of the meeting at Emmaus, reminding us that this is how we see Christ in everyday life, as an ordinary man, unrecognised. Rowan Williams has emphasised the significance of the image of the risen Christ not as 'a dead friend, but a living stranger'.[6] He also reflects on the 'enormous importance' of Christ's breaking bread with his disciples on three occasions after the Resurrection, the sharing of food and drink lying at the heart of Christian communion.[7] This is a Christianity that Bloomsbury could understand and respect. The picture was removed from its former location in 2005, at the request of local parishioners, to reveal the empty Victorian arcade behind. It must be said that it is not an entirely successful work and one can understand why the parishioners might not want it to dominate the altar space. Happily, its reminder of the significance of the landscape of the here-and-now in the context of Christian communion, is retained in its new location, against the east wall of the north aisle.

Vanessa, Duncan and Quentin are all buried not far away in the churchyard at Firle. Two severely plain adjacent gravestones simply carry names and dates, Vanessa's being slightly arched and of a hard dark grey-green stone, while Duncan's is shorter, of a browner stone and straight-topped. Charleston is less than half an hour's walk away, cutting across Firle Park and back along the ancient bridleway between fields along the foot of the Downs. Nothing could better explain why Bloomsbury came to Sussex, and stayed.

Getting there National grid ref. TQ515055
- The church of St Michael & All Angels is generally open in daylight hours.
- **Website:** http://www.acny.org.uk/4777/
- **By road:** Berwick is signposted on the right of the A27 Lewes to Eastbourne road between Selmeston and Polegate. The Cricketers in Berwick is an excellent pub serving good food.
- **Cycling:** View the National Cycle Network website: www.sustrans.org.uk
- **By rail:** Berwick is on the Lewes to Eastbourne line. The station is about half a mile (800 metres) north of the church. For train times phone the national enquiry line: 08457 484950.

BRIEF LIVES

Carrington, Dora *1893-1932*
Artist. Married Ralph Partridge in 1921. Companion of Lytton Strachey, and committed suicide after his death.

Fry, Roger *1866-1934*
Influential Cambridge-educated art critic, artist and sometime lover of Vanessa Bell. Pioneering apostle of modern art.

Keynes, John Maynard *1883-1946*
Influential economist and writer, sometime lover of Duncan Grant. Created 1st Baron Keynes of Tilton in 1942.

MacCarthy, Desmond *1877-1952*
Cambridge-educated writer and critic, knighted in 1951.

Partridge, Frances *1900-2004*
Pacifist writer and diarist. Second wife of Ralph Partridge (died 1960). Close friend of many of the Bloomsbury group, and frequent visitor to Charleston. Mother-in-law of Henrietta Garnett, daughter of David and Angelica Garnett.

Sackville-West, Victoria ('Vita') *1892-1962*
Writer and gardener, close friend of Virginia Woolf. Married to Sir Harold Nicolson (*1886-1968*), diplomat, writer and diarist.

Strachey, Lytton *1880-1932*
Cambridge-educated writer and first cousin of Duncan Grant.

Strachey, Marjorie *1882-1962*
Writer and teacher, sister of Lytton Strachey and cousin of Duncan Grant.

Sydney-Turner, Saxon *1880-1962*
Cambridge-educated civil servant and early friend of Virginia Woolf. The most elusive member of the Bloomsbury group.

A note on the Omega Workshops

Founded by Roger Fry in London's Fitzroy Square in 1913, with Vanessa and Duncan as fellow directors, the Omega Workshops included public showrooms and studios, and aimed to translate the excitement of modern art into the field of interior decoration. All work was anonymous, and artists were helpfully paid on a daily rate, thus providing welcome income for many often impoverished young artists.

BIBLIOGRAPHY

Judith Adamson (ed.), *Leonard Woolf & Trekkie Richie Parsons, 1941-1968*, Chatto & Windus, London, 2001.

Noel Annan, 'The best of Bloomsbury', *The New York Review of Books*, 29 March, 1990, pp.28-30

Quentin Bell, *Bloomsbury*, Weidenfeld & Nicolson, London, 1968.

Quentin Bell, *Virginia Woolf, A Biography*, 2 volumes, The Hogarth Press, London, 1972.

Quentin Bell, 'Recollections and reflections on Maynard Keynes', in Derek Crabtree and T.P. Thirlwall (eds.), *Keynes and the Bloomsbury Group*, Macmillan, London, 1980, pp.69-86.

Quentin Bell, 'Charleston', *Art Digest*, March 1981, pp.172-6.

Quentin Bell, 'Charleston preserved', in Quentin Bell, Anjelica Garnett, Henrietta Garnett & Richard Shone, *Charleston Past And Present*, The Hogarth Press, London, 1987, pp.7-16.

Quentin Bell, 'Charleston garden: a memory of childhood', in *Charleston Past And Present*, Quentin Bell, Anjelica Garnett, Henrietta Garnett & Richard Shone, The Hogarth Press, London, 1987, pp.84-104.

Quentin Bell, 'Charleston revisited', *Charleston Newsletter*, no.17, The Charleston Trust, June 1989, pp. 7-9.

Quentin Bell, *Elders and Betters*, John Murray, London, 1995.

Quentin Bell and Angelica Garnett, *Vanessa Bell's Family Album*, Norman & Hobhouse Ltd., London, 1981.

Quentin Bell and Virginia Nicholson, *Charleston: A Bloomsbury House & Garden*, Frances Lincoln, London, 1997.

Elizabeth Bowen, 'Virginia Woolf', in *Recollections of Virginia Woolf by Her Contemporaries,* Joan Russell Noble (ed.), Peter Owen Ltd., London, 1972, pp.47-53.

Caroline Dakers, *The Holland Park Circle: Artists and Victorian Society*, Yale University Press, New Haven and London, 1999.

Jane Dunn, *A Very Close Conspiracy: Vanessa Bell and Virginia Woolf*, Jonathan Cape, London, 1990.

Jane Dunn, 'Who's afraid of Vanessa Bell?', *The Guardian*, 13 Dec, 1990.

BIBLIOGRAPHY

A. Dunoyer de Segonzac, Foreword to catalogue, *Exhibition of Paintings by Vanessa Bell (1880-1961)*, the Adams Gallery, London, Oct 1961.

Angelica Garnett, 'Virginia Woolf', in *Recollections of Virginia Woolf by Her Contemporaries*, Joan Russell Noble (ed.), Peter Owen Ltd., London, 1972, pp.83-9.

Angelica Garnett, *Deceived with Kindness: A Bloomsbury Childhood*, The Hogarth Press, London, 1984.

Angelica Garnett, 'Charleston remembered', *The Antique Collector*, May 1986, pp.67-71.

Angelica Garnett, 'The earthly paradise', in *Charleston Past And Present*, Quentin Bell, Angelica Garnett, Henrietta Garnett & Richard Shone, The Hogarth Press, London, 1987, pp.104-53.

Angelica Garnett, 'The restoration of Charleston', *Charleston Newsletter*, no.23, The Charleston Trust, June 1989, pp.14-20.

Angelica Garnett, *The Eternal Moment*, Puckerbrush Press, Orono, Maine, 1998.

David Garnett, *The Flowers of the Forest*, Chatto & Windus, London, 1955.

Lia Giachero (ed.), *Vanessa Bell: Sketches in Pen and Ink* (1997), Pimlico, London, 1998.

Edmund W. Gilbert, *Brighton: Old Ocean's Bauble*, Methuen, London, 1954.

Lawrence Gowing, 'Remembering Duncan and Vanessa', in *A Cézanne in the Hedge and Other Memories of Charleston and Bloomsbury*, Hugh Lee (ed.), Collins & Brown, London, 1992, pp.32-8.

Christopher Green (ed.), *Art Made Modern: Roger Fry's Vision of Art*, The Courtauld Gallery/Merrell Holberton, London, 2000.

Jacquetta Hawkes, *Man and the Sun*, Cresset Press, London, 1962.

Jennifer Hawkins and Marianne Hollis (eds.), *The Thirties: British Art and Design Before the War*, Arts Council of Great Britain, London, 1979.

Diana Higgens, *Grace at Charleston*, Lewes, 1994.

Wendy Hitchmough, *Arts and Crafts Gardens*, V&A Publications, London, 2005.

Simon Houfe, 'Drawing inspiration/ How to get the look', *Homes & Gardens*, September 1986, pp.85-92.

Anne Kirker and Peter Tomory, *British Painting 1800-1990 in Australian and New Zealand Public Collections*, The Beagle Press, Sydney NSW, 1997.

Hermione Lee, *Virginia Woolf (1996)*, Vintage, London, 1997.

Fiona MacCarthy, *The Omega Workshops 1913-1919: Decorative Arts of Bloomsbury*, The Crafts Council, London, 1984.

Regina Marler (ed.), *Selected Letters Of Vanessa Bell*, Bloomsbury, London, 1993.

Louie Mayer, 'Virginia Woolf' in *Recollections of Virginia Woolf by Her Contemporaries*, Joan Russell Noble (ed.), Peter Owen Ltd., London, 1972, pp.154-63.

Richard Morphet, 'The significance of Charleston', *Apollo*, November 1867, pp.342-5.

Virginia Nicholson, *Charleston, an Artist's Home*, The Charleston Trust, Firle, 1999.

Nigel Nicolson, 'Vita and Virginia and Vanessa', in *A Cézanne in the Hedge and Other Memories of Charleston and Bloomsbury*, Hugh Lee (ed.), Collins & Brown, London, 1992, pp.86-93.

Mollie Panter-Downes, 'Charleston, Sussex', *The New Yorker*, 18 August, 1988, pp.60-67.

Frances Partridge, 'Bloomsbury Houses' in *A Cézanne in the Hedge and Other Memories of Charleston and Bloomsbury*, Hugh Lee (ed.) Collins & Brown, London, 1992, pp.128-36.

Christopher Reed, *Bloomsbury Rooms: Modernism, Subculture, and Domesticity*, Yale University Press, New Haven and London, 2004.

John Russell, 'A Bloomsbury founder, always with an idea', *The New York Times*, 7 March, 1997, p. C30.

Richard Shone, *Bloomsbury Portraits*, Phaidon Press, London, 1976.

Richard Shone, *The Berwick Church Paintings*, Berwick, revised edition, 1986.

Richard Shone, 'Official guide to the house and garden – introduction & the rooms and their contents', in *Charleston Past And Present*, Quentin Bell, Angelica Garnett, Henrietta Garnett & Richard Shone, The Hogarth Press, London, 1987, pp.17-81.

Richard Shone, 'Asheham: an outline history', *The Charleston Magazine*, Issue 9, Spring/Summer 1994, pp.36-41.

Richard Shone, *The Art Of Bloomsbury*, Tate Gallery Publishing, London, 1999.

Robert Skidelsky, 'Maynard and Lydia Keynes at Tilton', Charleston Newsletter No.7, 1984, pp.11-16.

Joanna Skipwith (ed.), *The Sitwells and the Arts of the 1920s and 1930s*, National Portrait Gallery, London, 1995.

Frances Spalding, *Vanessa Bell*, Weidenfeld & Nicolson, London, 1983.

Frances Spalding, *Duncan Grant: a Biography*, Chatto & Windus, London, 1997.

George Spater and Ian Parsons, *A Marriage of True Minds: an Intimate Portrait of Leonard and Virginia Woolf*, Harcourt Brace Jovanovich, New York and London, 1977.

Simon Watney, *The Art of Duncan Grant*, John Murray, London, 1990.

Simon Watney, 'Charleston', *Art Quarterly*, Summer 2005, pp.28-32.

Rowan Williams, *Resurrection: Interpreting the Easter Gospel (1982)*,

Darton, Longman & Todd, London, 2002.

Leonard Woolf, *Barbarians at the Gate*, Victor Gollancz Ltd., London, 1939.

Leonard Woolf, *Beginning Again: an Autobiography of the Years 1911-1918*, The Hogarth Press, London, 1964.

Leonard Woolf, *Downhill All the Way: an Autobiography of the Years 1919-1939*, The Hogarth Press, London, 1967.

Leonard Woolf, *The Journey Not the Arrival Matters: an Autobiography of the Years 1939-1969*, The Hogarth Press, London, 1969.

Rosemary Woolf, *The English Religious Lyric in the Middle Ages (1968)*, The Clarendon Press, Oxford, 1998.

Virginia Woolf, *The Voyage Out (1915)*, The Hogarth Press, London, 1927.

Virginia Woolf, *Orlando*, The Hogarth Press, London, 1928.

Virginia Woolf, *A Room of One's Own (1929)*, The Hogarth Press, London, 1977.

Virginia Woolf, *Between the Acts*, The Hogarth Press, London, 1941.

Virginia Woolf, 'Professions for women', *The Death of the Moth*, The Hogarth Press, London, 1942, pp.149-154.

Virginia Woolf, *Moments of Being, Unpublished autobiographical writings of Virginia Woolf*, edited by Jeanne Schulkind, University of Sussex/Chatto & Windus, London, 1976.

Virginia Woolf, *The Letters of Virginia Woolf*, edited by Nigel Nicolson and Joanna Trautmann, The Hogarth Press, London, 6 volumes, 1975-1980.

Virginia Woolf, *The Diary of Virginia Woolf*, edited by Anne Olivier Bell, assisted by Andrew McNeillie, The Hogarth Press, London, 5 volumes, 1976-1982.

Virginia Woolf, 'Asheham diary', *The Charleston Magazine*, Issue 9, Spring/Summer 1994, pp.27-36.

FOOTNOTES

Introduction
1. *Quentin Bell and Angelica Garnett, 1981*
2. *VW, 1942, p.86.*
3. *Noel Annan, 1990, pp.28-30.*
4. *Patti Smith, The Culture Show, BBC 4, June 2006.*

The Bloomsbury Group
1. *LW, 1964, p.21.*
2. *VB to Clive Bell, 14 June 1931, Letters, Marler, 1993 p.364.*
3. *VW, 1942, p.207.*
4. *Quentin Bell, 1968, p.42.*
5. *LW, 1939, p.31.*
6. *LW, Barbarians at the Gate, Victor Gollancz Ltd,*
7. *Quentin Bell, 1968, p.27.*
8. *Jane Dunn, 1990, p.241.*
9. *VW, 12 February, 1937, Diary, Vol.5, 1984, p54.*
10. *Angelica Garnett, 1972, p.85-6.*
11. *Frances Spalding, 1983, p.xv.'*
12. *VW, 1976, p32.*
13. *VW, 'Reminiscences', 1976, p.32.*
14. *VB to VW, 11 May 1927, Letters, Marler, p.317*
15. *Jane Dunn, 1990, p.258.*
16. *Nigel Nicolson, 1992, p.86.*
17. *VW, 1928, p.193.)*
18. *VB to Roger Fry, 21 [?] July 1912, Letters, Marler, 1993, p.121.*
19. *Skipwith, 1995.*
20. *A. Dunoyer de Segonzac, 1961, n.p.*

The Sussex Connection
1. *Frances Partridge, 1992, p.132.*
2. *E.W. Gilbert, 1954, p.116.*
3. *LW, 1967, p.14.*
4. *VB to Roger Fry, 5 September 1927, Letters, Marler, 1993 p.323.*

Firle & Asheham
1. *VW, 'A Sketch Of The Past', 1976, p.87.*
2. *Caroline Dakers, 1999, p.24.*
3. *VW, 'A Sketch Of The Past', 1976, p.64.*
4. *Personal communication, 13 December 1980.*
5. *VW, 1942, p.152.*
6. *Richard Shone, 1994, p.36.*
7. *LW, 1964, p.56.*
8. *ibid.*
9. *David Garnett, 1955, p.102.*
10. *VW, 1915, p.368.*
11. *LW, 1964, p.57.*
12. *LW, 1964, p.48.*
13. *Spater & Parsons, 1977, pp.75-82.*
14. *Spater & Parsons, 1977, p.90.*
15. *LW, 1964, p.60.*
16. *VB to VW, 19 August 1912, Letters, Marler, 1993, p.124.*
17. *VW, to Janet Case, 10 December 1914, Letters, Vol.2, 1976, p.55.*
18. *VW, 16 December 1918, Diary, Vol.1, 1977, p.228.*
19. *Richard Shone, 1994, p.38.*
20. *VW to VB, 10 [?] April 1913, Letters, Vol.2, 1976, p. 22.*

Monks House
1. *LW, 1967, p.13.*
2. *LW, 1967, p.16.*
3. *VW to Saxon Sidney-Turner, 11 September 1919, Letters, Vol.2, 1976, p.389.*
4. *VW, to Lytton Strachey, 14 September 1919, Letters, Vol.2, 1976, p. 390.*
5. *VW, 28 September 1919, Diary, Vol.1, 1977, p.302.*
6. *VW, 3 July 1919, Diary, Vol.1, 1977, pp 286-97.*
7. *Angelica Garnett, 1984, pp. 109-10.*
8. *Louie Mayer, 1972, p. 155.*
9. *VW, 9 June 1927, Diary, Vol.3, 1980, p.89.*
10. *VW, 26 August 1922, Diary, Vol.2, 1978, p. 195.*
11. *VW, 1928, p.170.*
12. *VW to Vita Sackville-West, 26 January 1926, Letters, Vol.3, 1977, pp. 231-32).*
13. *VW to Lady Robert Cecil, end February 1920, Letters, Vol.2, 1976, p.423.*
14. *VW to VB , 13 June 1926, Letters, Vol.3, 1977, p.273.*
15. *VW, to VB, end August 1927, Letters, Vol.3, 1977, p.415.*
16. *VW to Vita Sackville-West, 17 February 1926, Letters, Vol.3, 1977, pp.241-42.*
17. *VW to VB, 5 August 1937, Letters, Vol.6, 1980, p.153.*
18. *VW, 13 April 1929, Diary, Vol.3, 1980, p.221.*
19. *VW to VB, Letters, Vol.3, 1977, p.509.*

20. *VW to VB*, 7 April 1929, Letters,Vol.4, 1978, p.37.
21. *VW to VB*, 12 December [?] 1932, Letters,Vol.5, 1979, p.136.
22. Richard Shone, 1976, pp.243-44.
23. *VW to VB*, 3 February, 1931 [?], Letters, 1978, Vol.4, p.287.
24. *VW to VB*, 10 September 1931, Letters,Vol.4, p.377.
25. *VW to Mrs Ethel Grant*, 28 December 1937, Letters,Vol.6, 1980, p.198.
26. *VW to VB*, 28 December 1937, Letters,Vol.6, 1980, p. 196.
27. Angelica Garnett, 1984, p. 113.
28. Spater & Parsons, 1977, p.118.
29. LW, 1967, p.142.
30. Hermione Lee, 1997, p.4.
31. Louie Mayer, 1972, p.155.
32. ibid., p.160.
33. *VW to Marjorie Joad*, 15 February 1925, Letters,Vol.3, 1977, p.168.
34. Angelica Garnett 1972, p.85.
35. LW, 1967, p.112.
36. See Vanessa's 1925 design for a cushion cover, illustrated in the sales catalogue for Charleston Papers, Sotheby's, 21 July 1980, lot 210, n.p.
37. LW, archive, The University of Sussex Library.
38. ibid.
39. ibid.
40. *VW to Ethel Smyth*, 16 August 1940, Letters, Vol. 6, 1980, p.418.
41. *VW to Ethel Smyth*, 11 September 1940, Letters, Vol.6, 1980, p.430.
42. *VW*, 28 June 1940, Diary,Vol.5, 1984, p.99.
43. *VW*, 16 August 1940, Diary,Vol.5, 1984, p.311.
44. *VW*, 13 May 1941, Diary,Vol.5, 1984, p.284.
45. *VW, to Edward Sackville-West*, 1 December 1940, Letters,Vol.6, 1980, p.449.
46. *VW to Vita Sackville-West*, 19 January 1941, Letters,Vol.6, 1980, p.462.
47. *VW to Ethel Smyth*, 20 September 1940, Letters,Vol.6, 1980, p.433.
48. *VW to VB*, 25 September 1940, Letters,Vol.6, 1980, p.434.
49. *VW to Vita Sackville-West*, 15 November 1940, Letters,Vol. 6, 1980, p.446.
50. *VW*, 23 November 1940, Diary,Vol.5, 1984, p.340.
51. Hermione Lee, 1997, p.430.
52. *VW*, 19 December 1940, Diary,Vol.5, 1984, p.344.
53. *VW*, 29 December 1940, Diary,Vol. 5, 1984, p.347.
54. Hermione Lee, 1997, p.175.
55. Elizabeth Bowen, 1972, p.50.
56. Louie Mayer, 1972, p.162-63.
57. *VW*, 1928, pp. 284.

58. ibid., p.286.
59. The version in Australia by Duncan Grant is reproduced in Kirker & Tomory, 1997, cat.no. 820, p.92.
60. *VW to Mrs Ethel Grant*, 20 August 1938, Letters, Vol. 6, 1980, p. 266.
61. Nigel Nicolson, 1992, p.86.
62. *VW to Violet Dickinson*, 22 October 1937, Letters,Vol. 6, 1980, p.184.
63. *VW*, 24 March 1941, Diary,Vol. 5, 1984, p. 359.

Charleston
1. Quentin Bell, 1986, p.9.
2. Lawrence Gowing, 1992, p.3.
3. Personal communication, 20 April, 1991.
4. *VB to Roger Fry*, 4 September 1927, Letters, Marler, 1993, p.322
5. *VW*, 6 August 1923, Diary,Vol.2, 1978, p.260.
6. *VB to Roger Fry*, 16 October 1916, Letters, Marler, 1993, pp. 200-201.
7. *VB to Duncan Grant*, 3 August 1921, Letters, Marler, 1993, p. 253.
8. Lawrence Gowing, 1992, p. 37.
9. LW, 1964, p.27.
10. Frances Spalding, 1983, p.177.
11. *VB to Roger Fry*, 2 July 1911, Letters, Marler, 1993, p. 102.
12. *VW*, 'A Sketch Of The Past', 1976, p.126.
13. Angelica Garnett, 1984, p. 159.
14. John Russell, 1994, p.175.
15. Mollie Panter-Downes, 1988, p. 60.
16. Quentin Bell, 1981, p. 176.
17. Simon Houfe, 1986. See also Angelica Garnett, 1998, pp.101-11.
18. Angelica Garnett, 1984, pp.92-93.
19. Quentin Bell and Virginia Nicholson, 1997, p. 112.
20. ibid.
21. Angelica Garnett, 1986, p.71.
22. ibid.
23. *VB to VW*, 3 May 1913, Letters, Marler, 1993, p.138.
24. Wendy Hitchmough, 2005, p.6.
25. Simon Watney, 1990, p. 54.
26. Quentin Bell, 'Charleston Garden: A memory of Childhood', 1987 ; and Angelica Garnett, 1984 and 1987.

Berwick Church
1. Richard Shone, 1986, n.p.
2. Frances Spalding, 1997, p.384.
3. Angelica Garnett, 1998, p.38.
4. Jacquetta Hawkes, 1962, p.203.
5. Rosemary Woolf, 1968, pp.21-22.
6. Rowan Williams, 2002, p.74.
7. Rowan Williams, 2002, pp.98-108.

INDEX

Asheham House   6, 7, 27, 30, 31-7

Bell, Clive   7, 12, 30, 37, 67-8
Bell, Quentin
    Berwick church   81, 84, 86-7
    Charleston   57, 65-8, 70, 78
Bell, Vanessa   11, 26-7
    Asheham   6, 34, 35, 36-7
    Berwick church   80, 82-3, 84-6
    Charleston   7, 56-7, 65-6, 67, 68, 70, 71, 72, 73–5, 77
    Little Talland House   29
    Monks House   43-4, 53
Berwick church   7, 9-88
    the Annunciation   84-5
    chancel   86-7
    Christ in Glory   83-4
    the Crucifixion   86
    the Nativity   85
    pulpit   85-6
    rood screen   86
    the Supper at Emmaus   87-8
book covers   8, 21, 69, 71

Charleston   6-8, 18, 26, 48, 56-78
    decoration   57-60, 64-5, 67, 69
    garden   77-8
    paintings   36, 57-8, 66, 67-8, 70, 71, 72, 73, 74, 76
china/ceramics   53, 75, 76, 86

Embroidery   44, 58, 60, 71, 73, 74, 75, 87

Fabrics   68, 69, 73
Firle   6, 26, 28-30, 56, 88
Fry, Roger   10, 11, 12, 26, 89
    Charleston   37, 58-9, 67, 75, 77

Garnett, Angelica
    Berwick church   81, 83, 85
    Charleston   62, 68-9, 72, 75, 78
    Monks House   39, 44, 46
Garnett, David   33, 56, 61-2
Grant, Duncan
    Asheham House   36, 37
    Berwick church   80, 81-2, 85-7
    Charleston   7, 8, 56-7, 59, 65-8, 70-7
    Monks House   43, 44, 52

Hogarth Press   8, 21, 35, 44–5, 46, 49, 51

Interior design   7, 19-22, 58

Keynes, John Maynard   10, 12, 30, 34, 37, 70, 80, 82, 89

Little Talland House   28-30

Modernism   9, 17-23, 36, 58, 65, 71
Monks House   27, 38-55
    furnishings   7-8, 42-3, 52-3, 75, 76
    garden   41, 42, 54-5
    paintings   38, 53
Music Room exhibition   19, 43, 53, 73, 76

Omega Workshops   21, 36, 53, 68, 70, 74, 89

Strachey, Lytton   12, 30, 36, 39, 68, 89

Woolf, Leonard
    Asheham House   29, 34-5
    Monks House   7, 8, 41, 51, 54-5
Woolf, Virginia (née Stephen)
    Asheham House   6-7, 29-30, 31-7
    Little Talland House   28-30
    Monks House   8, 38-55